Information and
Communication
Technologies in
Everyday Life

Information and Communication Technologies in Everyday Life

A Concise Introduction and Research Guide

Leslie Haddon

Oxford • New York

English edition
First published in 2004 by
Berg
Editorial offices:
1st Floor, Angel Court, 81 St Clements Street, Oxford OX4 1AW, UK
175 Fifth Avenue, New York, NY 10010, USA

Berg is the imprint of Oxford International Publishers Ltd.

Library of Congress Cataloging-in-Publication Data
A catalog record for this book is available from the Library of Congress.

British Library Cataloguing-in-Publication Data
A catalogue record for this book is available from the British Library.

ISBN 1 85973 793 5 (hardback)
     1 85973 798 6 (paperback)

Typeset by JS Typesetting Ltd, Wellingborough, Northants.
Printed in the United Kingdom by Biddles Ltd, King's Lynn.

www.bergpublishers.com

Contents

Acknowledgements

I would like to thank Roger Silverstone at the London School of Economics for involving me in much of the original research that went into this book and for making valuable suggestions about my original proposal. Work for Ben Anderson at British Telecommunications plc and later Chimera, part of the University of Essex, helped to shape the format of the book and provided an opportunity to review much of the literature. It was his suggestion to develop a book from this project. Thanks, too, go to Ralph Schroeder, who has been extremely encouraging throughout. He also provided guidance and feedback on the original proposal. Richard Ling made a number of useful comments on the early draft. I appreciate the efforts of Annevi Kant as she not only checked through the work but also helped me in my goal of making this text accessible to a wide range of readers. Finally, thanks to my wife, Sue, for her patience and support.

1

Introduction

The aim of this book is to introduce research on information and communication technologies (ICTs) and everyday life primarily to students entering the field and to those developing these technologies and services. The book provides a guide to a number of the main existing research areas and poses some possible questions for future research.

Perhaps it is best to start with a clarification of the words used in the title. The term 'information and communication technology' dates from the mid-1980s and in particular from the British PICT initiative, a programme for looking at ICTs (Dutton, 1996). One glossary from the programme leader's summary of that work defined ICTs as 'all kinds of electronic systems used for broadcasting, telecommunications and computer-mediated communications' (Dutton, 1999, p. 7), while elsewhere he gives the examples of 'personal computers, video games, interactive TV, cell phones, the Internet [and] electronic payments systems' (Dutton, 1999, p. 3). This combination of general definition and examples conveys a sense of what ICTs can include, without having to draw absolutely precise boundaries. This might be just as well given the ongoing development of technologies and services.

Turning to the second key term, scholarly work looking at 'everyday life' in general has a longer intellectual heritage that can be traced back to Lukács and later Lefebvre and de Certeau in Europe and the Chicago school, Goffman and Garfinkel in the USA (Bennett and Watson, 2002). However, the study of 'information technologies in everyday life' is more recent. Hence, the book focuses mainly on the research undertaken since the 1990s. In practice, 'everyday life' has tended not to mean the whole of life. Instead, the studies have tended to deal with those parts of life outside the formal worlds of work and education.

The roots of empirical work in this field can be traced back to 1980s research on the social uses of television, on the (then new) home computer market and on the domestic phone. However, it was the 1990s that saw a substantial growth in commercial and academic research in the field of ICTs, research that was spurred on by a combination of factors. These included the plethora of new services and equipment that appeared, the most visible of which related to the Internet and mobile telephony. Many ICT companies developed a greater awareness of the importance of private users as a market. In particular, many telecom companies realized that they needed to know their markets better, especially following liberalization, privatization and the move to a more competitive commercial environment in European telecommunications. This meant that in addition to state-sponsored studies, social scientists could find another source of funding to conduct research.

A certain amount of the, now considerable, output from this research has been published in book form and in the journals that have emerged to cater for this new field. This is more so for British and American studies and for those researchers willing to write in, or have their work translated into, English. However, other contributions remain dispersed across a diverse range of journals, conference proceedings and papers given in workshops. Some studies have been published in various European languages – especially French, German and Italian studies – but have not yet appeared in English. Some research has not yet even reached the public domain. One aim of this book is to make more of this material accessible in one text and in English.

The increasing academic interest in the private use of ICTs is shown in the growing community of students and researchers coming from higher education courses in media studies and in communication studies and from courses such as innovation studies or those dealing with technology and society. Meanwhile, students of design and engineering, who will later be developing ICTs, often have modules addressing the social dimensions of these technologies.

As already noted, ICT companies, more so larger companies in practice (Haddon and Paul, 2001; Haddon, 2002), have acknowledged the need to know more about ICTs and the realities of everyday life. Hence the rise in the number of social scientists within these companies and the range of industry-financed reviews and studies conducted by universities, institutes or consultants.

The interest of policy makers has been reflected in the research they have supported, such as the various European telematics projects. Here we see concerns about the different forms of digital divide as well as hopes about the social inclusion that ICTs might facilitate. Nor are social inclusion and exclusion the only policy interests. Another example would be policy concerns about children's experiences on the Internet alongside a desire to promote their digital skills and literacy. Non-governmental organizations (NGOs) have also started to take an interest in this field for similar reasons.

In addition to the greater amount of research taking place, there has been an increase in its visibility and dissemination. There is more coverage of user research and indeed more journals devoted to the social aspects of ICTs.[1] Apart from this dissemination by publication, a number of networks of researchers emerged in the 1990s that also, sometimes informally, created a greater awareness of what research was taking place across countries within companies and academia. Finally, the 1990s saw the emergence of relevant conferences and other meetings on ICTs that have proliferated further in the twenty-first century. It is in the light of all these developments that it seemed timely to write this book.

The Theoretical Framework of Domestication

Alongside, and sometimes in conjunction with, the growth in empirical research we have seen the evolution and refinement of theoretical frameworks, tools and approaches. The central one providing the organizing principles for this book is that of 'domestication'. While the studies described in later chapters actually come from far wider traditions of research, it is this framework that constitutes the starting point for most of the analysis. Therefore it seems appropriate to provide some brief exposition of its history and key elements.

The concept, at least as applied to ICTs, emerged at the start of the 1990s from an empirical and theoretical project organized by Roger Silverstone at Brunel University. It was partly influenced by the emerging literature on consumption in general (Silverstone et al., 1992; Silverstone 1994; Silverstone and Haddon, 1996b). I became involved in the second stage of that project, which had by then moved to Sussex University. Here studies of teleworkers, lone parents and the young elderly enabled further exploration of how this approach might be applied. The studies also led to incremental development around its key themes (Haddon and Silverstone, 1993, 1995a, 1996).

The domestication framework was used by a wider European community of researchers partly because of the academic networks in this field that were forming in the 1990s (e.g. EMTEL, COST248, COST269). Norwegian researchers in Trondheim in particular played an important role.[2] In the UK, the framework was employed by the Sussex researchers in later studies for companies. It also formed a basis for some policy-related documents (Haddon and Silverstone, 1995b) and discussions of issues such as ICTs and social exclusion (Silverstone, 1995; Haddon, 2000b). The term now has an even wider currency and appears regularly in international papers on ICTs.

While many of the themes from the domestication framework will become clearer in the later section outlining the structure of the book, we can summarize some of its key features at this point. Most early statements on domestication, as well as most of the early British research, focused on social processes at work when new ICTs entered the home. The term itself evokes a sense of 'taming the wild'. These ICTs have meanings for people, people who individually and collectively also have a sense of identity. Hence domestication analysis considers what various ICTs symbolize, whether they are seen as a threat or are seen as somehow offering the possibility of enhancing social life. There is an emphasis on the social relationships surrounding ICTs. For example, it looks at the interactions between household members: their negotiation of the rules about ICT use, as well as tensions or even conflicts over that use. Once ICTs have crossed the threshold, part of the further process of their domestication involves physically locating these technologies in the home, finding a time for their use in people's routines and, in various senses, displaying their place in our lives to others.

If this was the initial starting point of the domestication framework, later British work in this tradition went on to examine the later careers of ICTs, how our relationship to them changed long after their initial acquisition. This research raised questions about extending the framework beyond the home, as will be reflected in later chapters. All in all, the approach provides a very useful way of exploring a social complexity beyond any simple 'benefits' and 'uses' of technology. Thus, while this book is not primarily intended to assess domestication, in general the chapters are organized from the particular interests of the author in this approach. Domestication provides an initial viewpoint from which to survey the field.

Choices within the Book

There are always limits to what can be covered in any one book. Some derive from the nature of the perspective itself. Because of its focus on social relationships, domestication in general does not consider the types of individual mental processes that might be associated with, for example, a 'uses and gratifications' framework. But then there are the particular interests and choices of the author. For example, although I have been involved in studies of the social shaping of technology and attempts to link that interest with domestication, this issue receives only a limited amount of attention in Chapter 9 on careers.[3] And while domestication writings have addressed questions of ICTs and the shaping of identity, including families' collective identities, this theme is covered only briefly, for example, in Chapter 4 when reflecting upon some of the claims made about gender.

However, at various points the book explores how the domestication approach can make contributions to different debates and it makes connections with other literatures as and when appropriate. For example, various chapters draw upon insights offered by studies of the life course, generational analysis, the social construction of experiences such as childhood and parenthood, analyses of public/private boundaries and the literature on the experience of time.

As regards the choice of ICTs that I cover in this book, the mobile phone and Internet receive the most attention. This reflects both general trends in recent research and the fact that these are areas with which I am more familiar. In terms of coverage, research on the fixed-line phone and on the computer comes next. It was my intention not to use the short space available to spend too much time discussing TV research, since this is an area that has already been well covered in media studies. However, I admit that a range of audio technologies, such as radio and MP3, as well as visual ones, such as digital cameras and camcorders, receive little or no attention. Yet, some of the more general social processes described in the book would in principle also apply to them. In this sense, they are not meant to be excluded from the general analytical framework.

A final set of choices relates to the national location of the studies covered. The majority of the research cited is European, partly reflecting the projects and academic networks in which I have participated. While the research agendas, cultural circumstances and history of ICT markets in these different countries may vary, my experience suggests that they also share much in common. Or at least they share enough for the purposes of exploring some of the themes of this book. However, I also look at North American research, especially when there are important debates that have received more attention there. And I cite studies from other parts of the world if I feel that they are relevant to the discussions of general social processes and issues. Specific information to contextualize those national studies is provided as appropriate.

Structure of the Book

There is more than one way in which the material reported in this book could have been structured and ordered. A number of researchers have specifically addressed issues around the digital divide and social exclusion. There is an increasingly substantial sub-literature on children, youth and ICTs. Both subjects therefore merited their own chapters rather than having the material dispersed across the book. However, they can also be treated as worked examples, a way to introduce themes and issues of more general interest, some of which can be followed up in later chapters.

This leads into a chapter that follows directly from the interests of domestication research: how we manage relationships around ICTs, especially but not only in the home. The domestication interest is then extended to consider social networks and ICTs, which is becoming an identifiable literature in its own right. The same is true of time and ICTs, while mobility and ICTs seems to be an emerging research area. All three topics have their own chapter.

There is enough material dealing with the dynamics of ICTs to justify two chapters. The first looks at how people's changing life circumstances affect their relationships to ICTs. The second deals with the careers of ICTs themselves and our relationship to them over time. One difficult decision was whether or not to have a chapter on gender and ICTs, which arguably could constitute another cluster of research in its own right. Ultimately, the chapter chosen was broader than gender, how we manage our relationships with others through ICTs. Inevitably, though, this is where one would expect to find some specific discussions about gender issues.

Because the same research could sometimes be relevant to more than one chapter, there is some cross-referencing to and reminders about studies described elsewhere in the book. The rest of this introduction outlines the chapter themes in a little more detail, relates them to the domestication framework and poses the questions that are to be addressed in the chapters. Each chapter then commences with a brief statement of those questions and the interests emerging from the domestication framework. Usually they do not consider domestication further, except in the chapters on social networks and mobility where part of the aim is to extend the framework.

Chapter 2

Questions concerning digital divides, haves and have-nots and social exclusion have been raised in policy and academic circles on various continents. While many relate to the Internet, they have also touched upon other ICTs.[4] Admittedly, concerns about the uneven distribution of ICT access and skills, uneven patterns of use and uneven levels of interest were not the key motivation for British empirical research on domestication. Nevertheless, this framework can provide some insights into the processes of adoption and the integration of ICTs into everyday life – or when and why this does not happen – that are clearly relevant for these debates. Starting with this issue of unevenness allows us to explore what counts as 'adoption', 'access' and 'use'. These are all measures that are crucial in much ICT research. Hence, we can reflect more broadly on a range of methodological issues as well as the problems involved in evaluating social consequences.

Chapter 2 starts by questioning whether we should think in terms of binary oppositions such as haves and have-nots when studying the uneven patterns of take-up and use of ICTs. It examines some of the problems associated with a variety of measures relating to this unevenness, before moving on to the specific evidence about an Internet digital divide. There has been some discussion of the consequences of unevenness, more often through statements of principle and hypothetical examples. Drawing both upon British empirical domestication studies and other research, the chapter reflects on what the presence and absence of ICTs mean to people in everyday life. In fact, if we consider the reactions of non-adopters, and especially former adopters, this can lead us to a more critical approach than often exists in those policy and commercial discourses. Many of these simply stress the benefits of online life and focus on (removing) barriers to adoption and use. Although much of the domestication analysis focused on the acquisition of ICTs and how they fitted into daily life, it always insisted that such adoption was not inevitable.

Chapter 3

The domestication framework looked mainly at children in terms of their role as household members, and how parent child relationships shaped negotiations around the place and experience of ICTs in the home. The ensuing empirical research considered in more detail parents' concerns about their children, attempts to control children's use of ICTs and children's resistance to those efforts. Thus, the material reviewed here provides an introduction to the broader theme of domestic politics. The final section of the chapter deals specifically with older children, with youth. Although it acknowledged the rest of social life, in practice the British empirical work looked mainly at processes within the home.[5] The literature on youth and ICTs allows us to start broadening the focus of domestication beyond the home and family, to consider the influence of peer networks (see also Haddon, 2003b)

Chapter 3 begins by providing a wider context to parent–child relationships. It examines the extent to which childhood and parenthood are socially and historically constructed. This is important because it shows how the experiences associated with these roles are not simply natural and universal. In fact, we will see how ICTs can become involved in the ongoing construction of what it is to be a child or a (good) parent. Next we consider how, in some countries at least, parent–child relationships are influenced by the arrival of new ICTs as well as by changes in the spaces where they are used. This leads on to issues of parental regulation of ICTs and children's reaction to that regulation. Moving over to the sections on youth, we find that young people are be no means identical in their use of ICTs. Yet, in various ways we can see how their orientation to peers at this stage in life shapes their take-up and use of ICTs as well as a range of related practices. We can also start to explore the communications choices we make from the repertoire open to us through considering the example of young people's prolific use of textual messages.

Chapter 4

Many marketing studies, as well as some academic research, emphasize the way in which individuals use ICTs, their perceptions, their attitudes, their practices, their styles and so on. One central theme of the domestication approach (as well as of a number of other forms of analysis) is that those individuals act in the context of other people, be they other household members, social network members, work colleagues or simply co-present others when outside the home. Therefore, some themes cut across many chapters. These include how other people influence the individual's experience of ICTs, how those others are affected by the individual's use of ICTs and how people as collectivities negotiate the experience of ICTs. These all raise issues of power and interpersonal politics.

Chapter 4 examines how, in a variety of ways, we manage relationships through and around ICTs. We have already seen some of these processes in Chapter 3 dealing with parent–child relationships. Now we start to explore others. The first section looks at efforts to control the use of the fixed-line phone. We then turn to examples of how interactions within the home relate to issues around gender and ICTs. This is followed by research on gender and managing relationships with the outside world, including relationships with the extended family. Lastly, the chapter considers some particular debates about the relationship between Internet use and sociability within the home, which will set the scene for a related discussion on sociability among social networks, a theme of the next chapter.

Chapter 5

The study of social networks has generated a literature in its own right. Networks have been of interest to those studying ICTs for a number of different reasons. Companies have been interested in the role that such networks play in the diffusion of new technologies and services. This diffusion can work through such mechanisms as word-of-mouth or through seeing the use made of ICTs by others within their social networks. Another tradition, of relevance to policy, has asked how social networks can provide people with social support, a theme that has found later formulations in terms of the amount of social capital we have and its effects on our quality of life. Do ICTs in general, and the Internet in particular, have a bearing upon this? One limitation should be noted here. The chapter will not address research on the Internet, community and civic engagement. While in some senses this could be seen as a continuation of work on social networks, this is one step too far removed from the primary interest in domestication.

Chapter 5 starts by examining how people first gain familiarity within, and even acquire ICTs through, their social networks. Subsequently those networks can go on to influence usage. While the domestication framework had originally concerned itself mainly with processes within the home, this chapter then makes the case for saying we might usefully stretch the concept to consider domestication processes among collectivities such as social networks. The second half of the chapter looks more specifically at discussions of social networks in relation to the Internet and the relationship between online and offline interactions. A number of, sometimes interrelated, debates concern the potential implications of the Internet for sociability among social networks. They ask whether the Internet influences who we interact with (e.g. does it change the balance of local and distant contacts), and they compare the 'quality' of online communication to other forms of interaction, addressing its ability to sustain social networks.

Chapter 6

Temporal considerations have always been an important part of domestication research, which has consistently asked about the way people manage time and how ICTs are fitted into their daily time schedules. Perhaps a less developed theme has been the difference that the arrival of ICTs might itself make to the way we organize time. More generally, the changing temporal patterns of our lives and the experience of time have been objects of study in their own right.

Chapter 6 starts by examining why the time spent using ICTs is an issue and for whom. Next it considers some of the domestication framework's interest in the time constraints that can have a bearing upon ICTs' adoption and use. Here we need to bear in mind not just overall disposable time but also the structure of people's time schedules. The chapter then moves on to subjective perceptions of time and how people's decisions about ICT use may be based upon those perceptions. Lastly, it deals with issues around ICTs' influence upon the way we plan time.

Chapter 7

While questions about domestic space featured in early British domestication research, people's movement through and presence in public spaces was not covered precisely because of the attention that was paid to the home.

Yet travel behaviour is clearly a part of daily life. Indeed, the experience of mobility is now attracting some attention as a topic in its own right. Research, in particular, on the use of the mobile phone when travelling around and in public spaces reminds us that we need to address mobility issues if we are to appreciate more fully our experience of portable ICTs.

Chapter 7 considers how we might assess the influence of changing mobility patterns upon ICT use, especially by considering the mobility of different groups in society and by disaggregating different types of travel. Still in somewhat speculative mode because of limited empirical data available, the chapter then considers the opposite relationship. It looks at how we might evaluate the influence of ICTs on mobility. Further sections deal with the consequences of ICTs for the organization of travel and for the subjective experience of travelling. The final section addresses the other main theme of the chapter, that of expectations and behaviour relating to ICTs in public spaces.

Chapter 8

Although the earliest statements about domestication emphasized the processes involved in the entry of ICTs into the home, follow-up research considered various transitions over the longer term (Haddon and Silverstone, 1993, 1995a, 1996). This is important because some of the researchers who have referred to the domestication approach see it as a process that can be finished. This question then becomes: has an ICT reached the stage where it is finally integrated into everyday life? End of story. The original proponents never saw such closure and so the empirical work noted above is used to chart ways in which the experience of the same ICTs can alter over time. Some of this is covered in Chapter 9 on the careers of ICTs, but Chapter 8 allows us to introduce the influence of changing life circumstances.

Chapter 8 illustrates the different dynamics experienced by individuals and households through a series of detailed examples. Studies of the move to unemployment and to teleworking provide examples of changes related to work. The example of the transition to single parenthood then introduces the effects of shifts in household composition. Standing back from such specific periods in life, we move on to reflect upon the more general evolution of gendered use of the telephone across different life stages, before returning to focus in on the specific changes associated with the birth of the first child and the transition to retirement. Finally, the chapter considers the issue of how much people's orientation to and decisions about ICTs reflect the conditions of their current life stage versus how much they reflect people's biographical experiences. Through looking at the case of the young elderly, we explore the effect of belonging to a certain generation or cohort of people with shared earlier life experiences. However, this is by no means a form of analysis that just applies to elderly people. Therefore, the chapter ends by reflecting upon the research questions this approach raises when thinking about generations of youth.

Chapter 9

The last topic involves a different set of dynamics. The entry of ICTs into the home and finding a place there were the key concerns of the very first writings on domestication. However, there are other traditions, especially those dealing with the history of ICTs, which can be drawn upon to expand our understanding of these processes. For example, the question of the relationship between newer ICTs and older ones, especially in discussions of whether they substitute for or complement each other, is a theme one finds within a number of strands of telecom and Internet research in particular. Meanwhile, changes affecting the longer term careers of ICTs have been explored in empirical research on domestication as well as in some North American research on the Internet.

Chapter 9 starts by looking at the factors shaping how people first learn about and perceive ICTs. This includes the influence of wider social discourses about those ICTs. More specifically, it includes the role of the media in shaping our awareness of technologies. As regards the question of how we learn to use ICTs, the chapter considers the sources of support in that process and the nature of experience with these technologies and services. Research on people's early experience of the Internet demonstrates how patterns of use change during that period. One long-standing interest of domestication research has been how new ICTs fit into the ensemble of artefacts that are already present in the home. Hence the chapter discusses how ICTs find a space in domestic environments. But 'fitting' into the home, or into our lives, also includes issues of how the use of newer ICTs is influenced by practices already established around older ones. This is then followed by the reverse question: how do new ICTs influence the consumption of existing ones? To answer this, the chapter explores the extent to which newer ICTs compete with, complement or introduce changes into the way we deal with older ICTs. The last section deals with the longer term careers of ICTs, examining some of the influences not already covered by households' and individuals' developing life circumstances. These include shifts in the wider public representations of technologies, changes in the nature of the technologies and services themselves, various ways in which adoption and use by others has a bearing upon people's consumption and the effects of adopting multiple versions of the same ICT.

Chapter 10

The conclusion reflects upon the domestication framework, its relations with other traditions of research, how it has and could be applied and how it can be extended. We then consider the general lessons that company researchers and students might draw from this book. Finally, as a worked example for students to reflect upon, we look at how the material in this book might be mobilized to evaluate the social consequences of ICTs.

Notes

1. If we take just the example of telecommunications research in Europe, in the 1990s the French journal *Réseaux* started to report more empirical studies of telecoms in everyday life. The journal *New Media and Society* appeared in 1999 and *Convergence* a little earlier.
2. For Norwegian examples, see Sørensen (1994), Berg (1996) and the collection by Lie and Sørensen (1996). For Dutch examples, see Bergman and van Zoonen (1999), Frissen (2000) and Rommes (2002). For Belgian examples, see Punie (1997) and Hartmann (2003). Ward (2003) provides an Irish example, and Frohlich and Kraut (2003) an American one. Lally (2002) in Australia and Bakardjieva and Smith (2001) in Canada have also drawn upon this approach.
3. Sørensen (1994) and Silverstone and Haddon (1996b) provide examples of papers trying to link the issues of design and domestication. For a more recent example of this approach, see Rommes (2002).
4. Discussed in Silverstone and Haddon (1995); also reported in Mansell and Steinmuller (2000).
5. Hartmann (2003) has noted that in this respect, Norwegian domestication studies have been more willing to look outside the home.

2

Uneven Patterns of Adoption and Use of ICTs

Concern over uneven patterns of adoption and use of ICTs has been reflected for some years in discussions of haves and have-nots. More recently, and specifically in the case of the Internet, we see this in discussions of the digital divide. In a European context the equivalent discussion has been in terms of 'social exclusion', although the older concepts of 'disadvantage' or 'deprivation' are also relevant.[1] Each of these terms operates within slightly different analytical frameworks. The primary interest in this field derives from the social agenda of the state, NGOs and those academics informing policy. There is a concern about the potential new forms of inequality that may arise through that differential take-up and use of ICTs. To take some European examples, we can see the EU TIDE programme addressing the potential problem that the very design of ICTs might itself exclude some elderly and disabled people from using them (Van Dusseldorp et al., 1998). Meanwhile, evaluations of telematics programmes ask if attempts to encourage ICT solutions might in fact lead to disadvantage for those who do not make use of these options (Silverstone and Haddon, 1995).

Although the prime driver of interest is policy, this unevenness is, or should be, also of relevance for ICT suppliers. For one thing, the launch of national and international (e.g. EU) telematics programmes in which companies are involved involves the state financing or otherwise supporting or promoting access to these new technologies. In addition, ICT developers have their own reasons for taking an interest in and understanding the uneven patterns of the market. These patterns can help them to make decisions as to whether some parts of the potential market are in practice unreachable because of people's resistance. By identifying who has and who has not acquired ICTs, along with current trends, they can try to determine where the market might develop or be developed next. On this basis, they can then change the technological offerings or marketing packages available in order to entice non-adopters to become adopters or to expand the usage of existing adopters.

This chapter will focus on uneven patterns of take-up within countries.[2] It first asks questions about ICTs in general. How appropriate is it to conceive of unevenness as a binary division, as implied by discussions of 'divide' and 'haves versus have-nots'? What are the ways in which that unevenness has been measured? What types of evidence have been cited? And what are the problems with these various measures?

Turning to the specific example of the Internet, what do different measures of uneven access to the Internet show and what is the evidence of change over time? What lessons can be learnt from general studies of social exclusion? What insights emerge from looking at the experience of older technologies, including those from domestication studies? Lastly, what can we learn from studies of non-users and former users of ICTs?

In terms of addressing a policy concern, this chapter sets the scene for understanding uneven adoption and use as one of the major issues relating to ICTs. Subsequent chapters enable us to appreciate further the factors that shape this unevenness. At the same time, the analysis provides a worked example. It aims to introduce some of the realities behind terms such as adoption and use, as well as show the complexities involved in measuring and evaluating the role and consequences of ICTs in everyday life.

Measures of Unevenness

Many researchers of both the Internet in particular and other ICTs in general would agree that it is questionable as to whether a binary division is adequate to capture the complexity that exists. For example, commenting on the results of a five-country European survey that looked at the ICTs possessed by European households (hereafter referred to as the Telsoc study),[3] one French analyst rejected such a simple dichotomy:

> Rather than talk about 'haves' and 'have-nots', as most official reports do, it would probably be better to talk about the distinction between individuals and households who are 'with it' and will have all the equipment and services, those who will only have part of them, and those again who will only have basic services (television and telephone). We must add those who have nothing at all to these three groups – even if they are few and far between. (Claisse, 1997a, p. 141)

He added in a later report:

> ...the processes of social differentiation are much more complex and cannot simply be explained away by a model of dualisation. Between households with only telephone and television and the 'super-equipped' households there is a

high degree of diversity and diversification of equipment combinations. (Claisse, 1997b, p. 34)

Next, we need to differentiate between access and possession since one can have access to (and use) a technology or service without actually owning it. For example, there is the practice of borrowing mobile phones. To provide some idea of the size of this phenomenon, in a European survey (referred to from now on as P-903), an average of 9 per cent claimed to have access to a mobile phone,[4] even though they personally did not own one, and this rose to 19 per cent in the Czech Republic, where the mobile market was less developed (Mante-Meijer el al., 2001).

Other qualitative studies have shown how social networks can also provide access to the Internet, for instance, by allowing friends to try out the Internet in their home (Haddon, 1999a). Internet cafés and libraries as well as institutions such as work and education provide further examples of how one can have access without ownership. The European P-903 survey found that more than 7 per cent of the European sample claimed to have access to the Internet outside the home even though they did not have a home subscription. This rose to 31 per cent in the case of the Czech Republic, where once again the Internet was less widespread. Clearly, these alternative sources of access can be important, more so in some countries than others, and lead to a slightly different picture of unevenness than that provided by measures of personal or household possessions and subscriptions.

Then there is the question of access within the home. People 'borrow' access to other household members' ICTs such as the mobile phone.[5] Or else they can use what is perceived to be a collectively owned device, such as the 'family computer'. In addition there is access by proxy. For instance, while not going online themselves, sometimes people get other household members to send and receive emails for them or look something up on the Net (Horrigan et al., 2003). Because of this some surveys have tried to ascertain whether a particular device is owned by someone within the household or whether it is accessible to other members.

However, one qualification here is that just because something is present in the home this does not mean that accessibility is straightforward. Qualitative studies have shown that access may involve a certain amount of negotiation. Sometimes there are constraints on – including rules about – use. We will see this explored in more detail in Chapter 3 when looking at parent–child relations and also in Chapter 4 on managing relationships. The point to make at this stage, though, is that when looking at any figures about the presence of ICTs in households, we have to bear in mind that social interaction in the home shapes how that 'access' is experienced in practice.[6]

Questions of access lead us on to the more general point that existing measures of adoption do not automatically imply usage. People may acquire but not use a technology. Conversely, some people may not be counted as 'adopters', even though they use particular ICTs. This is because they do not 'possess' them, but instead they have access to the technologies or services through other means. The European P-903 study attempted to accommodate this range of possibilities by distinguishing between the following groups:

1. Those who have access to the technologies and services and are current users (adopting users).
2. Those who do not 'own' the technologies or subscribe to services personally but who nevertheless have access to them and use them (non-adopting users).[7]
3. Those who 'own' the technologies or subscribe to services but do not use them (adopting non-users).
4. Those who neither have access to the technologies nor do they use them (non-adopting non-users).
5. Those who used to have access to the technologies and services and used to use them but no longer do so (former users or dropouts).[8]

(Mante-Meijer et al., 2001)

Several points can be made here. This typology refers only to adoption whereas in the light of the previous discussion we might also want to consider a typology including access rather than adoption.

Second, the fifth category shows that we may want to look beyond the snapshot of contemporary adoption and use to take into account previous adoption and use. Former users who have given up ICTs are different in social profile from those who have not adopted them yet and they may provide some clues about the problems that are encountered in using these products (Katz and Rice, 2002a). This group will be examined in more detail later in the chapter. But, to give some preliminary idea of the size of this group, the European P-903 survey at the end of 2000 found that 2 per cent of the sample were former users of the mobile phone and 5 per cent were former users of the Internet.

Third, is there a threshold below which we would be wary of claiming that someone is a user? For example, some people carry mobile phones 'for emergencies' and then do not make or receive calls. In one sense they can be considered to be 'using' the device – carrying it around provides peace of mind. But in terms of telephonic traffic, they are non-users. Or, if they have used the mobile for the occasional 'emergency' or contingency, they may be considered to be almost non-users. In principle the problem of how to handle rare use when trying to map the experience of ICTs can apply to other technologies as well. British researchers cited a UK survey showing that just over a quarter of 'users' had not used the Internet at all in the week preceding the survey. A further fifth had accessed it only once or twice (Wyatt et al., 2002). While not quite the same as the case of rare use, this does mean that we need to be careful not to read into adoption figures any over-optimistic assumptions about the frequency of use, and about the importance of ICTs in people's lives. As we will see, this is also relevant to the discussion at the end of this chapter, questioning people's commitment to the Internet.

Fourth, we need to take into account the technical nature of access (Thomas and Wyatt, 2000, reported in Rommes, 2002). For example, a Canadian qualitative study reported how the age, power and speed of the equipment installed in people's homes varied, reflecting their diverse motivations for going online and differences in how much money they were willing to spend (Bakardjieva, 2001). Meanwhile, a Dutch study made a related point, noting variations in modem and connection speeds (Rommes, 2002). These can all lead to users having different experiences of the Net, including differences in what can actually be accessed.[9]

Lastly, in many surveys usage is measured, in one way or another, by the time people spend using ICTs – as we shall see in the more detailed discussion of the Internet later. However, if we really want to know more about the uneven experience of ICTs we need to move beyond time (Jung et al., 2001).[10] For example, a variety of people could spend the same amount of time using an ICT but achieve different things. And 'heavier' use does not necessarily ensure more sophisticated use. In charting unevenness, some researchers are now asking how ICTs are actually used (Chen et al., 2002). They have asked about the degree to which people are able to 'use ICTs for personally or socially meaningful ends' (Warschauer, 2003, cited in Chen et al., 2002, p. 78). They have also raised questions about people's ability to use the Internet effectively (Jung et al., 2001, cited in Chen et al., 2002, p. 79). This entails considering measures such as users' different degrees of technological skills. Other researchers have asked how we should evaluate the quality of the Internet experience (Livingstone and Bober, 2003). They have suggested that we should consider the extent to which it is integrated into people's lives (Katz and Rice, 2002b). Finally, we would want to look into the consequences this might have for people's lives, even if there are a variety of criteria for evaluating those consequences. Compared to some of the earliest debates on digital divides there is clearly scope for a richer evaluation of unevenness. This is now starting to be realized.

Evidence about Uneven Access

Change over time

Although various North American studies of the Internet have shown that differences in use by standard socio-demographics continue to exist,[11] at least some studies have found that in the last few years certain gaps are closing. Examples would be the narrowing of gender and age divides (Katz et al., 2001; Chen et al., 2002; Katz and Rice, 2002b; see also Singh, 2001 on the Australian situation). The European P-903 study showed a similar closing of the gap both in relation to mobile phones and the Internet as the later groups of adopters included more older people and more women than the earlier ones (Mante-Meijer el al, 2001).

This is important because it can make evaluating the significance of any uneven patterns of take-up more complex. In fact, there is a somewhat common adoption process across many ICTs whereby the early adopters of innovations will often have one social profile but their domination of the market may be only temporary. If it is only temporary, how much should it be a cause for concern? Admittedly, there have been some criticisms of the extent to which we can simply assume a 'trickle-down effect', whereby innovations eventually reach wider audiences (Wyatt et al., 2002). For example, some groups continue to have many non-adopters even after the passage of time (e.g. the current generation of older elderly).

Illustrating the point a little further, where past precedents mean it is possible to imagine some reduction in unevenness over time, this can have a bearing on how unevenness is perceived as a problem, at least in public discourses. For instance, in the 1980s there was a widespread concern, reflected in media but also in some academic commentaries, over the gender gap in the early British home computer market. There were worries over girls being 'left behind'. Nowadays, when there is much less of a gender gap in access, this is not raised as the issue it once was. This is not meant to imply that there are now no questions to ask about gender experiences of computing. The point is, this forces us to reflect on how we interpret evidence of unevenness and on what becomes a public issue.

One final consideration is that among all the processes influencing any digital divide (and there will be multiple influences) the very object of adoption, in this case the Internet, is itself changing and evolving over time. Hence, if we do find that the socio-demographic composition of earlier and later diffusion groups differ, the later waves may not have delayed adoption because of some 'techno-conservatism'. They may simply be adopting later because the Internet has actually become more interesting, worthwhile and/

or easier to use or access compared to what it was when the early waves adopted it. The earlier waves may well have consisted of people who were willing to put up with more problems.[12]

Multiple Measures: Adding Further Complexity

We will now list some of the measures used in evidence specifically concerning the digital divide as it relates to the Internet. This will enable us to appreciate even better some of the potential complexity that is involved.

According to one US study, on any particular day, of all those who have access to the Internet, men, whites, higher income, higher educated and more experienced users are more likely to be online (Howard et al., 2001). This immediately underlines the fact that there are multiple measures of usage: 'use at all' (in answer to the question 'do you ever use...?'), 'regularly use' and in the above example, 'use on a daily basis'.[13] In addition, various studies (reviewed in Haythornthwaite, 2001b; Wellman and Haythornthwaite, 2002) point out that older users, although fewer in number than younger users, use the Internet for longer when they go online. In other words, we see yet another measure of usage: duration. Within that same review a further measure of usage that was discussed was the spread or breadth of usage – those who engage in more or less different kinds of online activities. If we no longer have a single measure of use but multiple measures, the binary digital divide might become an even more inappropriate descriptive framework. That is, unless all the measures indicate a trend in the same direction.

Some American researchers have pointed to yet further forms of unevenness in the market (Katz et al., 2001; Katz and Rice, 2002a, 2002b). First, they drew attention to the existence of a digital divide in terms of differences in the very awareness of the Internet (by age, gender and income). Second, they looked at the social composition of dropouts. Younger, less affluent and less well-educated people are more liable to become former users. This has important implications. To take income, in later diffusion waves more lower income groups were adopting the Internet, but at the same time more of those lower income groups were also dropping out. The overall result was that this particular gap was not narrowing.

Finally, as mentioned earlier, we need to consider what the Internet is used for. Consider the case of gender. Several studies have found differences in what males and females use the Internet for (Haythornthwaite, 2001b; Wellman and Haythornthwaite, 2002). If the Internet is itself composed of multiple elements (e.g. websites for viewing, transactional facilities, communication options) and if these have different roles in the life of males and females, or at least if there is a different emphasis, then in effect the Internet is a slightly different object for each sex. Moreover, if these patterns of use are different, how much weight should be placed upon figures measuring simple 'access' to the Net or total hours of use?

The Consequences of Uneven Access and Use

Why is unevenness of experience important? If we take the Internet as an example, some commentaries on the digital divide refer more generally to the argument that lack of access to the Internet might limit 'participation in society'. Others are more explicit and detailed, listing the ways in which non-users can be disadvantaged:

> inequities of awareness and use will be come increasingly urgent as more job-related services (postings of job opportunities, training), government functions and public service information (health education, insurance and financial support) become available via the Internet. (Katz et al., 2001, p. 416)

To start thinking about consequences of such unevenness, one first step is to review the lessons that can be learnt from some of the more general discussions of social exclusion. Second, we can consider the lessons from more detailed empirical studies of older technologies.

Lessons from the Social Exclusion Literature

In many respects, debates about social exclusion, as featured especially in EU discourses, are based on older discussions of 'relative poverty'. In particular they relate to discussion of 'relative deprivation', first promoted back in the 1960s.[14] One reason for referring to 'relative' poverty in those older debates is that poverty is a moving target over time. To be without certain possibilities at one point in time would not be considered such a major disadvantage in life. But once it becomes the norm to have those options, being without them can be perceived as being deprived. In principle, the same is true for social exclusion. And in principle, the same is true when considering ICTs. To an extent this is reflected in some of the commentaries made about the Internet. The argument is that there may be certain, limited, disadvantages now to not being online. But as more and more aspects of social life become manageable through the Net, as more communication takes place by email, as more and more people routinely use the Internet in everyday life, there is the increasing potential for non-users to become more disadvantaged in the future.

The other reason for referring to 'relative' when we discuss concepts like 'deprivation' is that disadvantage can itself be partial. We can be disadvantaged in some respects while not being disadvantaged in others. This moves us away from conceptualizing deprivation (or poverty) in terms of a single underclass and fits better with approaches within, for example, the literatures on gender, ethnicity, ageing and disability. In relation to our concerns in this chapter, it means that 'have-nots', or those on the wrong side of the digital divide, are not disadvantaged in every aspect of their life simply because of their lack of access to particular ICTs, even a multifaceted one like the Internet. They may be disadvantaged in certain respects, but not in others.[15]

Third, in the discussions of social exclusion and related concepts, access to resources, and especially economic resources, remains important. But they are not the only consideration. For example, two other important factors would be knowing what can be achieved online (a form of awareness) and having the skills and knowledge to achieve these goals (competence). These are not captured in measures of unevenness that focus solely on access (or more narrowly, on 'adoption').

Finally, one key concept in those original analyses of poverty in the 1960s was being able to 'participate' in society, joining in but also identifying with the social world. In fact, the very words 'social inclusion' have the merit that they capture this sense of avoiding social isolation. The implication is that we need to consider not just what we possess but also what we can do, the extent to which we can fulfil various social roles – which itself refers back to earlier discussions of social rights and of citizenship. Approaching the role that ICTs play in relation to social inclusion in this way would enable us to explore in more detail how the specialness of many ICTs, and by extension future ICTs, lies in facilitating connection with the wider society (Haddon, 2000b). This is especially so in the case of both the interpersonal and mass media of communication, which both practically and symbolically facilitate participation in the social and cultural world.

Lessons from Older ICTs

We now move from general arguments to the more detailed and systematic study of the place of one particular technology in our lives: telephony. The first example comes from a German study of unemployed people (Häußermann and Petrowsy, 1989),[16] and the second from a British article reflecting on studies of single parents and the young elderly (Haddon, 2000b).[17] All of these are reported in more detail in Chapter 8 on changing life circumstances, but for the purposes of this chapter, those findings can be summarized as follows.

There are some points that can be made very generally about the significance of access to telephony. They apply not only to the particular groups studied, but also to many other people. For example:

1. Those studies all showed how telephony has increasingly come to play a very important role in facilitating the logistics of everyday life, allowing people to be contactable quickly, to find out what was going on and to coordinate their interactions with others. In this sense we see how an interpersonal medium of communication helped to enable face-to-face contact and sociability.
2. The research also indicated how the telephone provided a significant channel of communication for maintaining involvement in family and social networks. In general the phone has become even more important to the extent that people increasingly operate over wider geographical areas and make contacts beyond the very local area. This in part derives from the degree to which greater residential mobility has dispersed both friends and kin.

There are some observations about the significance of telephony that may not apply to most people but which do apply to a number of people sharing related circumstances. For example:

3. The phone could take on an extra importance as a social lifeline for single parents looking after children in the evening and for those young elderly who were less mobile. Both these groups sometimes felt that they were trapped in home.
4. The telephone often played an important role by enabling psychological support for people coping with unemployment and for those single parents who had experienced the trauma of family breakdown.

Finally, there were instances where the phone had a particularly important role because of the specific circumstances of some groups. For example:

5. The phone helped unemployed people in a variety of ways, formally and informally, to increase work opportunities.
6. The telephone could be vital for helping single parents to manage any contingencies that arose (e.g. the child falling ill) when they were the only parent available to deal with them.

The first lesson from these examples is that in order to appreciate more fully forms of dependence and what it would mean to be without a commonly available technology, we really need to look beyond the broader arguments outlined in the previous section. We have to examine the detail of people's lives and how ICTs have come to fit into them. Moreover, it is important to take into account not just the generalities, the experiences common to many people. The particularities of different people's experience mean that ICTs can take on an added salience in life precisely because of those circumstances. Greater moments of dependency can result (with the single parents often commenting that the phone had proved to be a 'lifeline') as can a greater sense of loss or disadvantage if one has to do without a technology (as some young elderly found when the phone was accidentally cut off for a while).

We can extend these arguments beyond general telephony. Some of the points raised about telephony's importance for job opportunities and social networking could start to be applied to the mobile phone and the Internet. For example, the immediate contactability enabled by the mobile might be increasingly important for finding work. More generally as the mobile becomes ubiquitous in social life, new forms of disadvantage may be emerging for those without mobile telephony. Meanwhile, as a medium of interpersonal communication, research is already showing how email is starting to complement voice telephony in some social circles both for social messaging and for making arrangements. In some cases perishable information about what options are possible and what events are happening lends itself to distribution by email because of its one-to-many facility. Once again, we might ask for what purposes and at what stage in its wider diffusion might a lack of access to online messaging start to constitute a disadvantage? Can a lack of access mean that (new forms of) information passed around within social networks are missed? Or would the fallback of (fixed-line) voice telephony usually suffice?

However, we must also be a little cautious about overstressing the possible drawbacks of this lack of access. People show some ambiguity even towards technologies that they value. The best example is actually in relation to television in the single parent and young elderly studies (developed in Haddon, 2000b). Interviewees from both groups usually valued particular television programmes. More generally, TV was cheap entertainment when income was constrained or when people were tied to the home. It passed the time. It provided company. Most did not want to be without TV. On the other hand, many were critical of TV. They did not want it to dominate their lives. At many times, like the rest of the population, there were other things they preferred to do rather than watch TV. While there were slightly fewer criticisms of the phone, the costs of telephony could also create some concern or be an issue. Generally then, and in relation to all ICTs, if we want to understand both their adoption and their consequences for life we need to appreciate these negative aspects. The importance of this critical perspective is sometimes lost in discussions of the haves and have-notes.[18]

Studies on Non-users, Former Users and Intermittent Users of ICTs

In the course of collecting data about adoption and usage, surveys routinely collect figures on the non-adoption of ICTs, showing the socio-demographic profile of non-adopters. It was American researchers who first observed that non-adoption had only more rarely been studied in its own right (Katz and Aspden, 1998). Nor had former users or dropouts received much attention. Yet, given that advocates of the Internet emphasize the need to get on the bandwagon or else be left behind, any notable dropout rate here immediately raises suspicions about this claim (Wyatt et al., 2002).

British qualitative studies in the 1990s indicated that sometimes people exhibited active resistance to adoption of ICTs, revealing negative feelings about certain technologies (the 'resisters' in Wyatt et al's (2002) typology of non-users). Certainly TV-related products and services could evoke this response. For example, some people disliked the aesthetics of satellite dishes. Or else they were wary that putting a dish on the wall might imply to the outside world that they watched television all day. Large screens were sometimes avoided because that threatened to allow TV to 'dominate' the room. And some resisted the entry of cable into the home because it threatened to provide 'yet more TV' when there was already 'too much' (Silverstone and Haddon, 1996a).

For others, certain ICTs could be an irrelevance, never thought about because there were far more other important things in life that were taking up their attention. An example would be single parents coping with the pressures of marriage break-up, finding new housing, finding new work etc. (Haddon and Silverstone, 1995a).

However, those qualitative studies found that the most common reason given for non-adoption was actually that people said they simply had 'no need' for the device or the service. In line with a point made specifically concerning the Internet (Wyatt et al., 2002), some people do not want ICTs because they already have sufficient alternative sources of information and forms of communication. Belgian quantitative research also found 'no need' to be the most common explanation given for non-adoption, even before the cost of a product or service. Moreover, this researcher marshalled evidence to suggest that when people were saying they had no need for some technology this was not, for example, a smokescreen for the fact that they simply did not want to answer the question (Punie, 1997). 'No need' had become a common justification across many groups in society, although after some discussion of what it meant Punie argued that this response required further attention.

This theme reoccurred specifically in relation to the Internet. The P-903 European multi-country survey in 2000 showed little of the outright resistance to the Internet that was sometimes found in relation to the mobile phone (a negative reaction that had been discovered in the earlier 1996 five-country Telsoc quantitative study). Non-users of the Internet were more likely to exhibit indifference towards it rather than hostility.[19]

If we now turn from non-users to former users, the first article dealing specifically with Internet dropouts was based on US surveys in 1995 and 1996 (Katz and Aspden, 1998). The US researchers involved had been surprised to find that at that moment in time former users of Internet were as numerous as users (both 8 per cent of their sample). The researchers acknowledged that they had previously neglected this group because of their interest, shared with other researchers, in the rise of new ICTs rather than in their rejection. Yet, they argued that this rejection could reveal disincentives and barriers to use, as well as providing clues useful for designing and implementing an improved Internet.[20]

The researchers then proceeded to compare the profiles of users and former users. Some interesting results were that former users had been users for only a brief time (i.e. they had tried the Internet out), that teens were more likely to be dropouts and that there was very little difference in profile of teenage users and teenage dropouts. The major reason for giving up the Internet was loss of institutional access, as was the case in a comparison of surveys in later years. Other key factors were lack of interest, the complexity of the personal computer (PC), high costs and lack of time (Katz and Rice, 2002b). The impression arises that, despite claims about the existence of a young Internet generation, these teens, at this point in time in the USA, had a very casual relation with the Internet, not a committed one.[21] Further evidence of this casual relationship, true of older groups too but especially of teenagers, was that dropouts were more likely to have learnt to use the Internet informally, through friends and family. The authors pointed out that at this stage in life this teenage group also faced many competing attractions.

After reviewing some of the dropout data from the USA and UK, some British researchers conducted their own study of Northern Ireland university students who were about to graduate (Kingsley and Anderson, 1998). Hence this study focused specifically on the loss of institutional access to the Internet, asking students to evaluate the Internet and whether they would want to continue to have access after graduation through taking out a private subscription. The students were overwhelming less enthusiastic than some in the Internet industry would have desired. Once again they showed a high degree of indifference towards the online world. In fact, they did not foresee technical barriers to use, they were not critical of Web content and they did not convey particularly negative images when talking to other people about the Internet. But losing access was not felt to be a sufficient deprivation in their lives to make them actually want to pay to regain it.[22] The authors of this study observed that the years of using the Internet while at university should perhaps be better thought of as an extended free trial.

A later US study by Pew showed a flattening of Internet take-up, and the dropouts were increasing: in 2003 they constituted 17 per cent of all non-users. (The Pew Internet and American Life Project is a non-profit initiative that conducts regular surveys in the USA and funds analysis to explore the impact of the Internet.) As in the earliest study, about as many people were dropping out as were adopting (Horrigan et al., 2003). In keeping with the previous research already described, just over half said the main reason was a lack of need or desire, although admittedly a range of other factors were also mentioned.[23] The survey also observed that a substantial number of users were actually intermittent users who had gone offline for extended periods.[24] Again, a variety of reasons were given for this including losing of access or technological problems. But others cited social reasons in their lives (e.g. periods when they did not have enough time to go online). Or else they concluded that the Internet was simply not so useful to them at a certain time in their life. Such responses question the degree to which the Internet is integrated into users' lives. It also introduces the idea that the careers of ICTs generally can change over time, a line of analysis developed further in Chapter 9.

In sum, while there does not seem to be much active resistance to the Internet, some of the above evidence suggests that neither is it so attractive as those promoting the online world would have us believe. Even those on the positive side of the digital divide, i.e. users, appear to show at any one point in time differing degrees of commitment to the online world. In this sense, there might be some justification in critics challenging policy assumptions and the drive to provide access, referred to as the 'connection imperative' (Wyatt et al., 2002). These critics speculated that the ceiling on Internet growth might turn out to be lower than some forecasters had expected.

Conclusions

Dealing first with the policy issues, binary oppositions such as haves and have-nots and digital divides clearly do not do justice to the complexity of how the experience of ICTs is uneven. This has been shown not only in empirical studies charting the ICTs that people possess, but also in a typology bringing together multiple measures of uneven patterns of adoption and use.

As a worked example, the chapter has made a start in showing how measures of adoption, access and use can all be problematic. This will become even clearer in later chapters of the book when we look in more detail at the social processes relating to ICTs. One challenge for researchers entering this field is to ask themselves how many and what type of measures should be utilized in order to capture a richer picture of reality. Here, we have looked at the picture of the uneven experience of ICTs, but in principle it could be a picture of some other phenomenon relating to ICTs. The other side of the coin is that we have also seen how the existing methodological approaches already provide scope for debate as various analysts prioritize different measures. This reveals both the practical and theoretical decisions facing academic, policy-motivated and company-based researchers. In what circumstances and for what purposes should they retain multiple measures in order to develop a more nuanced representation of reality? Or when should they focus on fewer measures, choosing to prioritize some above others? They may want to do this in order to make new research comparable with existing studies so as to measure change. Or simplifying the picture may be a way to arrive at some overall judgement about the state of play.

Judging the consequences of a phenomenon such as the uneven experience of ICTs can be as difficult a challenge as measuring it in the first place. For example, by paying attention to the history of concerns about technology we saw that the degree to which uneven use is temporary can have a bearing on any such evaluations. Through reflecting upon the development of key concepts like social inclusion, it was clear that any disadvantage from not having access to or using ICTs can be relative and partial. Nor should we overlook empirical research revealing what ICTs mean to people. In relation to the digital divide debate, these studies showed how and why even those who use ICTs might also exhibit negative feelings about them, and how and why non-users and former users might reject them.

This all questions any assumptions that ICTs are always an unambiguously 'good thing', assumptions that technology simply means progress. As regards debates around the digital divide, it means we have to be cautious when assessing the view that some disadvantaged people in society are simply missing out. In general, researchers entering into the study of ICTs in everyday life need both to take a critical stance towards the subject matter and to chart the more detailed roles that technologies can play in our lives, sometimes considering the specific circumstances of different groups in society over and above more general arguments about the consequences of ICTs.

Notes

1. For a more detailed review see Haddon (1998b).
2. The global digital divide and factors shaping the uneven take-up between countries has been considered in, for example, Thomas and Mante-Meijer (2001) and Chen et al., (2002).
3. The Telsoc study was a survey conducted in 1996 for Telecom Italia and covered France, Germany, Italy, Spain and the UK. The results were published in Italian in Fortunati (1998).
4. Twice as many females claimed this. This study was conducted for EURESCOM, the research body jointly funded by European telecoms companies. The qualitative study conducted in 1999–2000 consisted of focus groups in the Czech Republic, Denmark, France, Italy, the Netherlands and Spain. The quantitative study in 2000 covered the Czech Republic, Denmark, France, Germany, Italy, the Netherlands, Norway, Spain and the UK.
5. This practice of 'borrowing' access also exists outside the home – as shown in Swedish research on the way in which young people borrow each other's mobile phones (Weilenmann and Larsson, 2001).
6. In this respect, one of the potentially pertinent developments is the trend towards multiple versions of ICTs within the home. For example, it is increasingly common to have multiple TVs and video-cassette recorders (VCRs), multiple phone handsets and multiple PCs, partly as individual household members acquire their own devices, partly as older devices are retained when upgrades enter the home. Arguably this arrangement sometimes provides greater freedom of use and of access, compared to the situation of having to negotiate with other household members over the use of a single TV, phone, computer, etc.
7. For example, the P-903 survey showed that by the end of 2000, 8 per cent of those surveyed were non-adopting users in the sense that they had access to the Internet only outside the home. If we compare this to the mobile phone, 9 per cent had 'shared access' – i.e. someone else in the household possessed a mobile that they could use.
8. Wyatt et al. (2002) make a further distinction within this category: the 'rejectors' who stop using the Internet voluntarily (e.g. because it was boring, because there were alternatives), and the 'expelled' who stop using it involuntarily (e.g. because of loss of institutional access).
9. Rommes (2002) argued that this could also lead to systematic gender differences, citing Dutch evidence showing that women had older computers and slower connections.

10. These researchers constructed an Internet Connectedness Index, taking into account a variety of factors and showed how more inequalities existed according to this measure than were shown by time measures (discussed in Katz and Rice, 2002b).

11. Reviewed in Haythornthwaite (2001b). See also Wellman and Haythornwaite (2002); Wyatt et al. (2002).

12. Wyatt et al. (2002) made another observation about the changing nature of the Internet itself. Later adopters may have joined the online world at a time when promotion of the Internet raised their expectations. This might have led them to be more disillusioned once the online world failed to live up to what they had imagined.

13. Wyatt et al. (2002) call for a more refined way of distinguishing between different types of user because of the range in frequency of use.

14. More details on the issues involved in processes of social exclusion and new telematics in general can be found in Haddon (1998b, 2000b) and also in Mansell and Steinmuller (2000), which draws heavily upon these studies.

15. For example, some may be relatively wealthier, lead comfortable lives, and feel no need for this technological option.

16. This article was based on a review of the existing German literature on the unemployed, on survey data and on official statistics.

17. The fieldwork for the study of single parents was conducted in 1993 and involved twenty parents filling out week-long diaries and then taking part in in-depth interviews. This was reported in Haddon and Silverstone (1995b). The study of the young elderly (here operationalized as 60–75 year olds) involved a further twenty participating households, with diaries and in-depth interviews. The fieldwork for the young elderly study was conducted in 1994 and reported in Haddon and Silverstone (1996). Both reports are available at http://members.aol.com/leshaddon/Date.html.

18. Wyatt et al. (2002) take such a view, listing the problems and deficiencies of the Internet that could severely diminish the attractiveness of the Internet experience.

19. Some initiatives designed to encourage more take-up of the Internet can be informative in this respect, even if they are only small-scale studies. Women taking part in a Dutch Internet training course had done so because they wanted to find out more about the online world – they feared being left behind. After the course, they decided that the Internet did not fit into their lives, but they were nevertheless happy that they had followed the course so that they could evaluate the Net – and become more 'informed rejectors' (Rommes, 2003).

20. A related point is made by Wyatt et al. (2002).

21. One qualification to add is that this evaluation was based on an analysis of the Internet at a particular point in time. Teenage relationships to the online world may change – e.g. following the greater entertainment possibilities after 'Napster' (comment by Richard Ling). That said, a British qualitative study of children's views of the Internet noted that, despite enthusiasm for it, many preferred to do other activities and use other media, 'seeing the Internet as something to use on "rainy days"'(Livingstone and Bober, 2003, p. 28).

22. The authors observed that at the time, loss of email access was not so significant since email was mostly used to contact other students, who were also about to lose email access.

23. These included, among other things, concerns about safety and unsavoury content, cost, lack of time, and the complexity of the Internet.

24. In their March–May 2002 survey 44 per cent were intermittent users. The figure was 27 per cent in their December 2002 one.

3

Children, Youth and ICTs

The digital divide is not the only area where there is a considerable public interest in the consequences of ICTs. As ICTs from the TV, through videos, games and computers to the Net have appeared, so there has been a history of concerns about the effects on children. Yet at the same time some technologies have been perceived as holding out the promise of better options for future generations. Or at least they may change in the experience of children and youth, for example by affecting their degree of independence.

To set the scene, this chapter first draws attention to the literature describing how the very experience of childhood and youth changes over time, regardless of the influence of ICTs. The expectations of what young people of different ages can and should do, their circumstances, the legal frameworks within which they operate, etc. have changed historically. In these senses childhood and adolescence are social constructs. So too is parenthood. This certainly provides a broader context within which to understand contemporary parent–child interactions. But more generally it reminds us that we can ask similar questions about any groups we study, not just parents and children, specifying how the experiences of that group are historically shaped.

Given the interest of domestication research in how the relationship between people affects the experience of ICTs, the focus then moves to parent–child relationships,[1] and how these may be changing. In particular, there are discussions, perhaps true of some countries in the developed world more than others, of children's media-rich bedroom culture and children's activities in supervised spaces. How has this had a bearing upon parents' ability to monitor children's use of ICTs? How interested are parents in controlling that use, what strategies do they employ to do so and how do children resist those strategies? Through looking at parents interacting with children, we are drawn into the core theme of Chapter 4 on how relationships around ICTs are managed, when there are different perspectives among family members and some conflicts of interest.

The section on youth starts by addressing some general stereotypes con-cerning young people's communications. To what extent are young people heavy telecoms users? How much variation exists in their telecoms behaviour, including gender differences, at this stage in their lives?

The central interest of much research on youth and ICTs relates to their peer orientation. Hence the chapter asks how peer relations influence the use of technologies like the Internet and mobile phone. How, for example, have teenage peer relationships shaped the use of text messaging and related practices? When do we need to pay attention to peer obligations or expectations about appropriate use? And how do fashions among peers have a bearing upon perceptions and choices of ICTs? Such discussions more broadly pave the way for thinking about the influence of social networks, gift-relationships, ICT-related practices beyond narrow definitions of 'use' and the symbolic meanings involved in acquiring particular ICTs.

Finally, as we have more communication options in our repertoire, one research question concerns how we choose between them (Haddon, 2003a). Of course, this will vary according to social groups' circumstances. But we can at least start to consider what type of considerations may be relevant through looking at young people's use of textual messages via the mobile and email.

Childhood, Youth and Parenthood as Historical Social Constructions

The Social Construction of Childhood and Youth

The 1990s saw a growing literature on the social construction of childhood. The key point is that the experience of children and youth as well as expecta-tions of their roles, their independence, their knowledge etc., are relative and change over time (e.g. see James and Prout, 1997). Sometimes change is gradual, taking place over hundreds of years, such as movement away from regarding children as simply small versions of adults (Ariès, 1973). The emergence at the end of the nineteenth century of the concept of adolescence as a stage between childhood and adulthood would be another example of such shifts in perception (Gillis, 1981).

Because such changes are relatively gradual it appears that successive generations have similar experiences. But there are also the more short- to medium-term changes. For example, in Britain the 1980s saw a lengthening of the period during which young people are financially dependent upon the family. This was because of the longer time spent in both education and training due to the pressures to acquire qualifications and from youth unemployment.

It is worth noting that in these discussions of social construction, the exact details of how childhood and youth are changing are themselves debated. For instance, one view is that there has been a move from children having autonomy and responsibility to being more protected, making fewer decisions and experiencing more restrictions in their daily activities (Vestby, 1994). Another view is that we see more autonomy experienced by children, more domestic democracy and the individualization of childhood – but also increased regulation and risk management of children by adults (Livingstone, 1997 – referring to Anthony Giddens' analysis). These two characterizations cover some similar points, but they are not identical.

Changes such as those shown in the examples above provide a wider context in which to appreciate parents' and children's contemporary behaviour. But we also have to take into account changes in expectations of children's consumption of ICTs and developments in their experiences of these technologies. For example, in different time periods (and in different cultures)[2] we might anticipate variations in adults' understanding of how children will make sense of media images or content, as well as their views about what children have to be protected from or can be exposed to. We have a more concrete illustration of changing expectations in a study commenting on Norwegian debates about the minimum age that children should be to have access to a mobile phone (Ling and Helmersen, 2000). After the mobile had spread widely among the teenage population, the new phenomenon in the late 1990s was mobile acquisition by pre-teens. This created some unease, as shown in interviews with parents about the age at which it was appropriate to have a mobile. In fact, even some contemporary teenagers commented that nowadays children were receiving mobile phones when they were 'too young', given that these young people had acquired a mobile themselves only when they were first in their teens. A number of participants thought that the start of secondary school was a better time for children to have their first mobile. The researchers added that during this period in the late 1990s the mobile phone became an 'appropriate' coming-of-age gift for children, suggesting a broader social (though perhaps temporary) fixing of the correct age for the consumption of this technology.

Yet children are not simply passive in this whole process. Part of the changing experience of childhood is that children are always growing up with new ICTs. In one British study we are reminded that children can themselves play an active role in the changing conditions of childhood 'through their imaginative responses, their creative play, their micro-practices of daily life [and their] pioneering of new media practices' (Livingstone and Bober, 2003, pp. 6–7).

The Social Construction of Parenthood

There has been less study of the social construction of parenthood, although it has been referred to by some in the literature on media (Buckingham, 1991; Vestby, 1994). In parallel with the preceding discussion of the social construction of childhood, to talk of parenthood as a social construct means that the experience of parents can all change somewhat over time. This includes their expectations of what counts as being a 'good parent', the expectations they feel they should have of their children and how they should approach the parental role. For example, one claim is that there is now an ideology of parenthood implying that parents should have a more detailed involvement in their children's lives, including an increasing expectation that they should protect their children from the flow of impressions and experiences (Vestby, 1994). It has been argued that this has altered the very process of growing up.

On the other hand, in parallel with one of the arguments made about the social construction of childhood, other writers emphasize that the family has become less authoritarian, a development which has received some attention especially in French studies of ICTs (Jouet, 2000). More democracy and effort to involve children in decisions may partly explain the greater leniency shown in efforts to control children's use of ICTs such as the TV (Pasquier, 2001).

However, these processes constructing what good parents should be like are not monolithic in their consequences. We can see this in examples of media use, where parental control varies by country. One cross-national study showed that parents in Sweden and Italy were less strict and rigorous than both those in Belgian Flanders and those in France. Parents in the first two countries had more lenient parenting styles, granting more freedom to children and this included their approaches to regulating children's media use (Pasquier et al., 1998). There is also variation within countries. For example, British studies have shown that working-class parents regulate their children's TV watching less (e.g. Buckingham, 1991) and a more recent European study of children has shown the similar influence of socio-economic status across countries (Pasquier, 2001).

As in the case of childhood, we can also see people being active in the very process of constructing parenthood. For instance, one Israeli study of people's views about the mobile phones pointed out how, through their complaints about children's use of the mobile, they were actually constructing what appropriate adult behaviour should be like. They were at the same time indicating how 'good parents' should control their children's use of their mobiles (Lemish and Cohen, 2003).

The ways in which new pressures on parents affect they way they deal with ICTs has been addressed in a number of writings. Some claim that there are now higher expectations than in the past that parents should spend 'quality time' with children, which can translate into spending time watching TV with them. Since the early 1980s many parents have felt the expectation that they should acquire microcomputers so that their children should not be 'left behind' (Haddon and Skinner, 1991; Skinner, 1994). In the 1990s, parents experienced a similar sense of guilt that led them to provide their children with Internet access (Haddon, 1999a). At the same time there have been discussions of how much parents should be expected to provide guidelines for their children's use of the Internet, both in the sense of making their children aware of safety issues and supporting their children's online literacy. And to the extent that parents sometimes find this task to be difficult, the further question arises as to what means could be found to support parents in managing their parental role (Livingstone, 2001).

Parent–Children Relationships and ICTs

Bedroom Culture and Activities in Supervised Spaces

There appears to have been a number of interrelated shifts in the experience of many children, in the West at least, that are relevant for understanding children's relationship to ICTs. One change is related to arguments about children's greater absence from unsupervised public spaces (Büchner, 1990; Livingstone, 2002). It has been argued, perhaps truer in some Western countries than in others,[3] that many social activities that in the past took place in public are increasingly taking place in the home. The home is itself becoming more public, more open to outsiders (Wellman, 1999). Children also experience this, having their friends around to interact with in their homes, in their own rooms (Livingstone, 2002).

This socializing in the home has been identified in a European study of children as 'bedroom culture'. Observing that this is a European and North American phenomenon, partly depending on wealth, this research showed the high proportion of European children, especially teenagers, who had their own room (e.g. 82 per cent of 15–16 year olds). Indeed, the majority of 15–16 year olds claimed to spend at least half their waking life in their rooms (Livingstone and Bovill, 2001a).

A number of factors shape this experience besides general affluence, some more country-specific than others. For example, in Britain the influence of the lack of leisure alternatives for children and youth outside the home has been commented upon (Bovill and Livingstone, 2001). In addition, the 1980s and 1990s have also seen the process, again perhaps true in some countries or areas than in others, whereby there has been a growing concern for children's safety in public spaces. The UK study of children and ICTs described how parents felt under pressure to keep their children indoors (Livingstone and Bovill, 1999; Livingstone 2002). Reflecting these concerns, we now have a situation where the vast majority of children in Britain are now driven to school.

However, children's mobility is complex. They spend time not just in their own homes but also in those of their friends. Although this is less well documented, one German study observed that certainly middle-class children spent a fair amount of time in organized post-school activities (Büchner, 1990). In this context, the European P-903 study commented upon the practice across countries of parents ferrying their children around to their friends' homes and to various events and activities (Klamer et al., 2000).

These are the background developments against which we can appreciate children's relations to ICTs. If we return to the bedroom culture, the researchers in the European study of children observed how children's bedrooms have become increasingly 'media-rich'. Children have gained more and more access to various personalized ICTs. In the 1960s (to take the dates relating to Britain) children, especially teenagers, increasingly acquired their own record-players and radios, which in later years evolved into music systems. Since then many children have been provided with or acquired their own TVs, VCRs and PCs.

This multiplication of ICTs within the home and their individual possession is at one level a solution to the domestic competition for communal resources. Different household members, including children, want to watch different programmes, to access computers or even to make phone calls at the same time. But in more recent years the practice of granting children access to a range of personal ICTs also reflects the need to provide alternatives if children are to be kept off the streets (Livingstone and Bovill, 1999). That said, parents do not always approve of these personalized ICTs, especially of television. But some nevertheless recognize the positive benefits. For example, personal ICTs allow and maybe encourage children to be more autonomous. Indeed, if children have their own personal ICTs this can mean that the parents have more privacy as well as choice – for example, when watching TV (Bovill and Livingstone, 2001).

Turning now to communications, British studies showed that by the 1990s some children had started to acquire their own fixed-phone handsets. Although the European study of children found that such personal phones were still rare, at the extreme end almost half the children in Sweden had them and in Israel and Italy 40 per cent of the children surveyed had their own phone handsets (D'Haenens, 2001). We have seen more examples of children accessing the Internet from their own rooms, although that same study showed that Internet access in children's bedrooms is still by no means the norm, being true only for under 10 per cent of households (D'Haenens, 2001).

Mobile phone sales have benefited from concerns about the times when children are out of the home, if only by offering parents some peace of mind. Sometimes this has been the reason why parents initially provided their children with the technology, although Norwegian studies have also pointed out that some parents have occasionally resisted acquiring mobiles for their children for what they see as the unjustified purpose of status display (Ling and Helmersen, 2000).

Parents' Concerns about Children's ICTs

The issue of the surveillance of children by parents is most clearly seen in the history of what type of and how much domestic television children were allowed to watch. Therefore, although similar issues have reoccurred with the arrival of videos, video games, home computing and more recently the Internet, we can probably get some idea of what is generally important to parents through looking at their reaction to TV.

British studies in the 1990s found that many parents were not so worried by particular concerns about content on television. It was more important to influence children's viewing in order to achieve some kind of 'balance' in the children's lives. They did not want their children to neglect some activities, including socializing with peers, at the expense of others. Using the metaphor relating to food, parents want children to have a 'balanced diet' (Livingstone, 2002), which was one reason for parents regulating the overall time that their children spend watching TV, using the PC or being online (Haddon, 1999a). The European study of children and screen media reached a similar conclusion. Although content was a public issue, and hence in a sense part of the social construction of what parents should be attentive to, it was actually not so much of an issue in private. If anything, it concerned mostly younger children. There was more regulation of time spent watching TV where it was felt to distract children and youth from other activities like sleep and homework (Pasquier, 2001). In the USA, equivalent parental concerns have been voiced about the amount of time teenagers spent on the PC in general (Frohlich et al., 2001) and on the Internet in particular (Lenhart et al., 2001).

Apart from this time issue, parents' concerns about children and the Internet have been characterized in terms of content, contact and commercialism (Livingstone, 2001; Buckingham, 2002; see also Lenhart et al., 2001 for the USA). 'Content' clearly relates to some of the same long-standing concerns about what children might encounter on television – such as sexuality and pornography. Because it is unregulated, another type of Internet content that has been highlighted is material found on race-hate sites. Clearly some parents are worried about these various types of content. But there seem to have been relatively few studies measuring in more detail the level of parental concern and who exactly is concerned about what (an exception being one Israeli study).[4]

Although receiving less attention in the popular media, researchers also examined some parents' apprehensions about commercialism on the Internet (Livingstone, 2003). This covers not only children's exploitation by advertising (Lenhart et al., 2001) but also the fear that marketers are targeting children online in order to get information about the family (Turow and Nir, 2000). A British study of children and screen media commenting upon the fact that parents were concerned about commercialism noted that worries about adverts creating the desire in children to buy things were actually greater than concerns about television violence upsetting children (Livingstone and Bovill, 1999).

As regards 'contact', British domestication studies in the 1990s already showed the interest that parents had in monitoring children's telephone behaviour. Parents sometimes wanted to know who their children were speaking to on the phone. Being conscious of phone bills, some parents preferred such phoning to take place in locations where the phone's use could be monitored. As a result, in certain households there were attempts to deny children the use of the phone handsets or cordless phones in private spaces like bedrooms (Haddon, 1997a).

One Norwegian study made a similar point. Some parents did not allow their children to have a mobile phone because they wanted to oversee the children's activities (Ling, 1998). More generally, concern about paedophiles has created some parental anxiety about their children making contact with strangers online.[5]

Yet by no means all parents are so restrictive as those in some of the examples given. We will see that allowing children private access to telecommunications has sometimes been viewed as a way of allowing them to take a step towards independence. There were additional benefits from allowing children their own handsets, phone lines or mobiles – such as relieving parents of the job of having to pass on messages to their children.

Parents Monitoring Children

For many children surveillance by parents has increased. This is because in their leisure time children are often either in the home or at other supervised locations. But in other ways, direct surveillance by parents of children's ICT use in general has become more problematic.

Bedroom culture has itself created some practical problems as regards monitoring media use (Bovill and Livingstone, 2001). So too has the arrival of new technologies. One French study observed that in contrast to the TV, but as in the case of the original home computer, many parents are acquiring access to the Internet at home for their children without themselves having a developed knowledge of what is possible via the Net (Lelong and Beaudouin, 2001). Moreover, even when parents had some experience of the Internet, their children often used it in different ways from the parents. For example, children more frequently used facilities like instant messaging and chat, with which the parents were less familiar. The researchers went on to point out that (besides creating problems for monitoring children) this meant that many parents were not in a strong position to influence their children's use of the Net, apart from broadly negotiating the maximum amount of time that children should spend online. A related point is made in the European study of children and screen media. With new technologies parents cannot rely on their own childhood experiences when making rules about use (Bovill and Livingstone, 2001).

The arrival of the mobile phone has also somewhat complicated parental surveillance. On the one hand, it offers more monitoring potential of a certain kind. Parents can phone to check up on their children when the latter are out of the home. In this sense, the mobile has been referred to as a 'digital leash' (Ling, 1997), although teenagers sometimes allowed such parental surveillance simply in order to gain possession of a mobile phone (Green, 2001). Sometimes teenagers accepted parental arguments about safety as being legitimate (Green, 2001). Yet at other times they resisted such monitoring (e.g. by diverting the calls sent to them by the parents directly to the mobile phone's voice mail – Ling and Yttri, 2002).[6]

The mobile phone has in other senses further increased children's capability to organize their social life beyond the surveillance of parents (Ling and Helmersen, 2000). While from the viewpoint of parents, this decreases their ability to monitor children's communications, from the viewpoint of children, it increases their own privacy.

Children Becoming Independent

As part of a larger French project examining the theme of youth gaining independence ('autonomization') one study emphasized how important the phone was in the processes by which young people gained autonomy, although children's use of the phone also led to tensions (Martin and de Singly, 2000). These arise not only because of the cost of calls made by young people (to be discussed in more detail in Chapter 4 on managing relationships) but also because of the time lost in making calls that could have been used for studying (from the parents' perspective). Some young people participating in that French study referred to this tension as 'the war of the telephone', a conflict between the pressure on youth to be attentive to the family and to their studies versus the demands by young people themselves for a zone of liberty of movement and expression. In principle, the vast majority of parents agreed with the need for youth to move progressively towards independence, but at any one time the degree of independence wanted by young people did not always match that wished by their parents.

This process of becoming independent is not solely a matter of conflict. If we return to the theme of bedroom culture described earlier, a Norwegian study viewed children's self-contained media-rich bedrooms as a way of parents gently allowing children's emancipation (Ling and Thrane, 2001). In a similar way, providing mobile phones can be a gesture through which parents offer children more independence. It allows young people a discrete space, even if an electronic one, enabling parents and children, for example, to check in with each other when the latter are exploring new spaces (Nafus and Tracey, 2002).

More generally, Norwegian researchers saw adolescents' adoption of mobile phones as one defining episode among others in the process of becoming independent, a chance to get a 'foot in the door of adulthood' (Ling and Helmersen, 2000, p. 23). In particular, paying for one's own mobile phone calls was seen as a symbolic confirmation of adulthood.[7] Meanwhile, those same studies argued that, although the mobile phone has now spread to the pre-teens, it was still easier for parents to justify teenagers having a mobile as their schedules and interactions became more complex and as they moved around more compared to when they were younger (Ling and Helmersen, 2000).

Parental Strategies for Controlling Children's ICTs

Methodological issues create problems as regards assessing parental control of children's ICT. For example, many studies have drawn attention to differences between children's and parents' reporting of how much parents regulate what programmes and how much television their children can watch. In a British study 75 per cent of mothers claimed to regulate their children's TV watching whereas only 41 per cent of children said they did; meanwhile 73 per cent of fathers claimed to do so whereas the children reported that only 35 per cent of the fathers regulated what they watched (Livingstone and Bovill, 1999). Qualitative research has suggested the same differences, reflecting the fact that some parents try to give the 'right answer' as 'good parents'. The same is true for the Net. US research has indicated that there are already gaps between parent's and children's reports of how much parents supervise children's Internet use (Lenhart et al., 2001; National School Boards Foundation, 2001). Obviously the more pressure there is for 'good parents' to control Internet use, the more this particular problem of measuring that regulation may arise.

Meanwhile, in various studies parents themselves observe that one strategy of control, relying on outside institutions to regulate media, has become less of an option with the proliferation of media channels (with video, satellite etc. that children could access, for example, at friends' homes) and with the arrival of what is perceived as being the unregulated Internet

If we turn now to details of how parents actually try to influence their children's use of ICTs, we might again learn some lessons from more established media such as TV. One British study underlined how parents preferred talking to children about TV rather than actually attempting to constrain children's viewing. In that study, the first approach used by parents was what has been termed 'evaluative'. This entailed discussing particular programmes with children to show them how to make sense of what they were seeing. The second most popular strategy was 'conversational', which entailed a more general discussion of programmes. 'Restrictive' strategies, i.e. limiting children's viewing, came only third (Livingstone and Bovill, 1999).

In a later study of young people's use of the Internet by the same researchers, examples of restrictive regulation included limiting the time that children could spend online, installing filtering software,[8] keeping the password secret so that the parent had to be called if the child wanted to go online, and banning or blocking certain activities such as email and chat. Examples of what the researchers call 'unobtrusive monitoring' included positioning the PC in a public place within the home, spot checking from time to time on what the child was doing and checking to see what sites had been visited (Livingstone and Bovill, 2001b). This strategy of unobtrusive monitoring has also been popular in the US (Frohlich et al., 2001; Frohlich and Kraut, 2003). In one survey by the American Pew organization, over two-thirds of computers used by young people to access the Internet were located in a space such as the living room, study, den or family room as opposed to one-third being located in a private bedroom (Lenhart et al., 2001).

As regards the mobile phone, Norwegian qualitative research described how parental control was a process of constant negotiation (Ling and

Helmersen, 2000). Here one particular issue was cost, with parents and children negotiating how usage would be financed, a negotiation itself influenced by the arrival of prepayment tariffs (Ling and Helmersen, 2000).

In the light of all these options open to them, how anxious are parents? This is difficult to evaluate, and will vary by ICT and according to the state of contemporary moral panics (or public concern). But in the case of TV, while parents have spoken of the difficulties of effectively restricting children's viewing, it is worth noting that they were often not so worried about children watching unsupervised in their bedrooms. Many regarded their children as being sensible and discriminating media users (Livingstone and Bovill, 1999). In the case of the Internet, a US study indicated that overall parents were satisfied with children's use and trusted their children when they explored the new medium (National School Boards Foundation, 2001).

Children's Resistance to Parental Controls

What of the children's perspective? If we return to the example of television, British studies have shown that despite parental attempts to influence what their children watched on television, the children themselves gained social status from watching adult material on TV (Buckingham, 1991, 1996). More generally, qualitative studies in France and Italy have also stressed how children do forbidden things as a way of showing that they are grown up – and this applies equally to media consumption (Pasquier et al., 1998).

Given various reasons why children have a different perspective from parents, it is not too surprising that a number of studies have documented children's strategies to access programmes that their parents did not want them to watch or to watch for longer than their parents preferred. Hence, accounts of children's resistance to regulation by parents have been characterized as an ongoing 'guerrilla war' (Buckingham, 1991), with children frequently 'avoiding' rules (Pasquier et al., 1998; Pasquier, 2001) and seeking to escape surveillance (e.g. by watching when parents were not around or by watching at someone else's home).

In general, we see some of the same themes emerging in relation to other ICTs such as the mobile phone.[9] For example, while in certain senses young people collaborated with parental monitoring of their behaviour through the mobile, in others they resisted it. Sometimes they developed 'parent management strategies', such as giving excuses like 'the battery ran out' when they made themselves uncontactable by their parents (Green, 2001). Meanwhile, a Japanese study described a phenomenon also found elsewhere, whereby youth often made an effort to keep their parents 'in the dark' about the content of their personal emails and voice calls (Ito and Daisuke, 2003). All the youth involved in that study preferred calling friends on mobiles rather than the home phone, despite the higher cost of doing so.

Finally, as shown in British research, children sometimes found parental monitoring to be an invasion of their privacy or their personal space, which could leave them frustrated. Once again, they employed a variety of tactics for evading this control, enjoying the challenge of outwitting adults (Livingstone and Bober, 2003). If we look at the USA, the Homenet study found that the 'contention for computing time is a heated issue in many of the families we visited' and sometimes could lead 'to an atmosphere of deception and mistrust' between parents and children (Frohlich and Kraut, 2003, p. 153). To give an idea of the scale of conflicts over ICTs, in one US survey 40 per cent of parents said that they had had arguments with their teenage children about the latter's use of the Internet (Lenhart et al., 2001). The American research underlined the fact that parents think there are far more dangers associated with the Internet than do their children.

Youth, Peers and ICTs

Youth as General Telecoms Users

Since a number of studies have emphasized the particular importance of telecoms to youth at this stage in their life, we can start by addressing some common assumptions about the degree to which teenagers make calls on the traditional phone line. One early US study suggested that teenagers dominated the phone and that they were the heaviest users in households (Dordick and LaRose, 1992). However, the problem with taking such results at face value is that these claims were based on the evaluations and perceptions of parents – which may not totally correspond to reality. As we shall see later in Chapter 4 on relationship management, parents may evaluate the calls of their children as being unnecessary or think they make too many calls for their age. Such assessments can influence parents' estimates of their children's usage.

In fact, a small-scale study researching teenagers in Australia challenged the stereotype that teenagers in general were heavy users (Skelton, 1989). Reviewing earlier US studies, Skelton agreed that teenagers with boy- or girlfriends could generate calls of long duration. And there was often a peak in phone calls when teenagers initially came home from school. Yet overall, teens did not generate massive amounts of calls. Various French studies would tend to support her view, indicating that younger as well as retired people actually use the phone less than the 25–60 age group (Claisse, 1989; Perin, 1994).

More recently, a French study has tried to distinguish different patterns of phone use among youth (Martin and de Singly, 2000). The researchers developed a typology from the survey data consisting of four categories. The first was those young people who were very family-orientated, who experienced a high level of parental control (which they accepted) and a low level of sociability with friends. They used the phone least. The second group consisted of those who experienced completely the opposite situation, and used the phone a good deal. The third group were the youth whom parents tried to control, but who did not always accept parental rules. They were very sociable with their peers and used the phone the most to evade parental control and stay in touch with their friends. Finally there were those whose parents did not try to exercise so much control, who simply enjoyed being at home, in their own rooms and who had a low sociability score. They used the phone less than the second and third groups.

The chief point to derive from this research is not so much the detail of the study (since, in general, different empirical studies might throw up slightly different typologies). More important is the finding that there is a certain amount of heterogeneity among youth. In the Martin and de Singly (2000) study we can see that differences in the experience of teenagers can arise from various factors such as home- versus peer-orientation, degrees of parental control, differing reactions to this etc. – all of which can influence telecoms behaviour. In a similar fashion, when discussing the use of screen-based ICTs, various writers have underlined the differences among youth both in terms of more standard socio-demographics and related tastes, values, attitudes and orientations (Buckingham, 2002) and in terms of other factors such as media styles (Bovill and Livingstone, 2001; Livingstone, 2002). Appreciation of this variation is sometimes missing in discussions of youth in general.

Finally, and as part of the ongoing reflection on gender through this book, there is the question of whether boys and girls have fundamentally different patterns of communication. The evidence has been mixed. Early French research found that among schoolchildren and teenagers there were few gender differences in the balance between 'intrinsic' (social) and 'instrumental' (functional) calls. These differences did not emerge until student days and were consolidated only in adulthood (Claisse, 1989). However, later Norwegian research found that teenage girls made longer calls and even at this stage the girls were developing a different style of communication compared to boys. The latter reported that they 'gave messages' when making calls, whereas the girls reported 'chatting' (Ling, 1998). Once again, we can see some of the systematic differences in communications that are starting to occur among young people.

Participating in the Peer Group

The early Australian study of teenagers first drew attention to the significance of the phone for sustaining interaction with friends outside school time (Skelton, 1989). This theme of youth using telecoms to manage participation in peer groups has been recurrent in research ever since. Notwithstanding the heterogeneity noted earlier, in general it has been argued that this is a period in life when the social networks of many young people are growing and when it is important to 'be available' to peers. In fact, being rung up is a measure of popularity (Ling, 1998; Ling and Yttri, 2002). Therefore, if we want to understand the adoption and use of this new technology at this stage in life it is important to look beyond individualistic decisions in order to appreciate 'individuals aligning themselves with the peer culture in which they participate' (Ling and Helmersen, 2000, p. 20).

US Internet studies have described how young people used instant messaging not only to arrange meetings or to talk to friends who were online at the same time, but also to hear if anything interesting was 'happening'. There were parallels with previous generations spending time in certain public spaces, such as a shopping mall, waiting for something to happen. They now appeared to be 'hanging out' online (Rainie, 2001). Both US and British studies have pointed out that some teenagers kept this channel open while doing other things on the computer, such as homework (Lenhart et al., 2001; Livingstone and Bovill, 2001b). Peers also exchanged addresses of websites that they had found as well as images captured from the web. They sometimes created mini-networks online by linking home pages via hyperlinks. And they influenced each others' value judgements, for example in terms of deciding what it was worth going to see on the Web and what counted as a good website address (Millerand et al., 1999).

In many countries the mobile phone has also become a tool to support peer networking. Indeed, for some young people the mobile phone was especially useful precisely because of the amount of time that they were out of the home at this stage in their life, when they could not be easily reached by the fixed-line home phone (Ling, 1998). Because of this, a number of Norwegian youth commented that nowadays they would be out of touch if they did not have a mobile and they would not 'know what is happening' (Ling and Yttri, 2002). In general, and enhanced later by the use of text messaging, the mobile has created more moment-by-moment awareness of what other peers are doing.[10]

Text messaging reflected that same ongoing effort made by young people to maintain a place in their social networks, as they asked questions such as 'what's happening, what's going on?' As in the case of voice calls, the number of text messages received was itself a measure of one's popularity, as was the number of names in the dialling register (Ling and Yttri, 2002). When they did not receive messages young people could now feel excluded and rejected – they felt that something was wrong (Taylor and Harper, 2001b).

A certain amount of messaging was undertaken for practical purposes, such as arranging a rendezvous, inviting people to a party, asking what's on at the cinema, etc.[11] But the purpose of other messages lay not so much in the content but rather in the act of having made contact. Teens reinforced a bond through demonstrating that they had thought of someone enough to send them a message, to give them the gift of a call. A similar observation has been made in a British study of email communication by young people. The content of messages can be repetitive and trivial but the main point sometimes appears to be keeping in touch rather than communicating information (Livingstone and Bovill, 2001b).

In this vein, a number of European studies have commented on youth texting as a 'gift relationship' (e.g. in the UK, Nafus and Tracey, 2002; in Norway, Johnsen, 2003).[12] Coming from an anthropological tradition, this approach sees gift-giving and gift-receiving as an activity for cementing the social relationships between people. When applied to youth, their rituals of exchange – though the mobile in general as well as texting – can provide a way of 'demonstrating and testing out the trust that exists in their relationships' (Taylor and Harper, 2001b, p. 18). For example, one British study described how the very act of leaving a mobile phone around on the table, so that friends can pick it up and explore its features, can represent an expression of trust in others. Then there is the practice of allowing others to use one's phone to make calls.[13] In fact, sometimes young people talk of feeling obliged to make their phone available to friends, otherwise they would be thought less of. Later, the person who borrowed the phone has to return the favour either in kind or by another means (buying credit for the friend's phone, buying a meal) (Taylor and Harper, 2001b).

Gift-giving, then, entails the obligation to reciprocate. We can see this in the case of text messaging. When young people sent messages they expected an answer, often straight away (in contrast to the argument that because text involves asynchronic messaging people can answer when it suits them).[14] Thus, we have examples of young people phoning up to ask 'what's wrong' when they did not get a reply to their text message, asking why they were being ignored. As the researchers put it, the recipient of the message was 'obliged to meet the challenge of the donor' (including answering messages that arrived in the early hours of the morning when they were asleep!) (Taylor and Harper, 2001b, p. 11).

Peer orientation is also highlighted in what could be called 'communication-related practices'. These are the activities that go beyond 'using' the technology in the sense of sending a message or making a call (Haddon, 2003a). One example would be showing a message to a friend, which in itself was an act of sharing, of gift-giving and which helped to reinforce that friendship (Taylor and Harper, 2001b; Kasesniemi and Rautianen, 2002 on observing Finnish youth). It may involve actually sending the message to the other person's mobile. In fact, this can happen even when the young people concerned are talking to each other at the same table, as they go through the ritual of saying when they have sent messages to, or received them from, each other. Of course not all messages are shared. Nor are all messages shared with everyone. Some are so transitory that they lose their meaning quickly when seen out of context. Others are too personal or risky to show (although sharing personal messages can create added intimacy). But certain messages are capable of being made more public among peers, like jokes.

However, just as there were understandings about (and attempts to influence usage of) ICTs within the family, various rules exist among peers about texting. There are perceptions of what is the right and wrong way to go about things. For example, even though texting often does not involve the use of formal grammar there, some young people objected to the overuse of capital letters or the lack of any punctuation, which could make messages difficult to read.[15] And there are understandings about when it was inappropriate to use texting as opposed to using other means of communication. An illustration of this would be when young people thought that it was not right to end a relationship, to 'dump' someone, through sending a text message (Taylor and Harper, 2001b).

Lastly, we can appreciate the influence of peers on young people's decisions through considering the role of fashion.[16] Norwegian research has argued that at one point in time it became fashionable for young people to have a pager not just because of its functionality but because having the device itself symbolized belonging to a group. Later the mobile phone was acquired because of this symbolic role (Ling, 1998). Yet, fashion considerations did not merely influence the decision to possess a mobile. They also shaped perceptions of what brands of mobiles were appropriate, the desirable age and size of models and, indeed, the choice of operator whose network was being used. These were all ways of demonstrating 'street cred' (Taylor and Harper, 2001a). Being aware of such factors was part of the successful mastery of personal display (e.g. it was not 'cool' to show off) (Green, 2001; Ling and Yttri, 2002).

Youth and Communication Choices

We now turn to the question of how people choose from their communications repertoires through looking at the case of young people sending and receiving textual messages. Sometimes, that decision relates to the fact that other communications options, such as mobile calls, are blocked. This itself shows us why it is worthwhile taking a holistic view and considering all the communications possibilities when we want to make sense of choices. In perhaps a rather extreme example, but one which shares some common elements with other countries, Japanese researchers have argued that mobile email in Japan was popular among young people partly because of the strong regulation of voice telephony in schools and public places (Ito and Daisuke, 2003). In schools, where mobiles tended to be officially banned, young people nevertheless used their mobiles (under the desk) to pass on emails illicitly during lessons. The prohibition was equally strong in many public spaces. One could find many 'no mobile phone' signs in trains and buses and there were regular announcements to this effect. As a result, almost none of the participants in this study made or received voice calls in these settings, but instead used mobile email extensively.

Turning to more positive reasons for the choice of text, part, but only part, of the popularity of text messaging among many youth lies in its low cost (relative to speaking on the mobile phone). Given the financial circumstances of many young people and the need to be frugal when they take responsibility for their telecoms bills, both analysts and teenagers interviewed across a range of studies have commented on the importance of the economic considerations (Fortunati, 2001; Johnson, 2003; Ling and Yttri, 2002). In addition, the price of a text message entailed a fixed cost, known in advance, whereas how long a phone call might take, and hence its cost, was not known so precisely. Hence texting appealed because it allowed young people to have a more detailed knowledge of and control over their expenditure.

The more intrinsic virtues of texts can be seen in the literature dealing with young people and dating. For example, one Norwegian study described the ritual whereby, after meeting face-to-face, young people often exchanged mobile numbers. This was sometimes followed up with a text message, perhaps asking a question or making some non-committal remarks as a way of showing interest in someone. Resorting to text could avoid having to deal with the embarrassment and fluster that can occur in a face-to-face approach (Ling and Yttri, 2002). A British study made a related observation about young people using the Internet for dating (Livingstone and Bovill, 2001b). In the USA, 17 per cent of participants in one survey had asked someone to go out with them via instant messaging (IM) and 13 per cent had broken up with someone through an instant message (Lenhart et al., 2001).

The advantage of text, be it text messaging, email, IM or whatever, is that it can allow teenagers the time to compose what they want to say carefully, especially if it involves delicate matters (Kasesniemi and Rautianen, 2002).

To use Goffman's framework, they can 'arrange face' and even to confer with a jury of their peers (Ling and Yttri, 2002). Several researchers have drawn attention to the fact that text messages sent through whatever medium allow young people to put into writing things that they would not dare to say aloud (Fortunati, 2001; Lenhart et al., 2001; Kasesniemi and Rautianen, 2002; Ling and Yttri, 2002).

Finally, a number of researchers have drawn attention to the advantages of the actual language used by young people when texting or sending instant messages. In the case of texting, the creative use of language and signs was admittedly due in part to the amount of space available for writing messages and the effort involved in keying in messages on a mobile phone. However, the use of codes can also exclude older generations from understanding them – acting as a kind of slang with in-group meanings (Taylor and Harper, 2001a; Ling and Yttri, 2002). In fact, it has been pointed out that sometimes this can also provide good camouflage for illicit practices such as sending messages in class (Ling, 1998). A related point has been made about teenage use of the Internet – that some teens use a form of language, a code, which marks their identity when chatting online (Millerand et al., 1999).

Conclusions

By starting with the social and historical construction of childhood and parenthood, we can ask what factors influence certain judgements that adults, especially parents, make. These include deciding the 'appropriate' age or stage for children to have access to different ICTs, to certain content or to a particular medium of communication. What shapes parents' beliefs about the way in which children experience and make sense of the world and what counts as 'maturity' in different contexts? How do judgements change over time about what children should do or be exposed to, as in the example given earlier of the mobile phone being adopted by pre-teen children? What influences expectations of how parents should behave? Given that parents are not passive in this process, to what extent do parents resist these discourses and on what grounds do they do so? To what extent and in what areas are they unclear about how to act? When do they feel guilty? What sources of support or guidance do they seek to manage their role as parents? And with what success do they do so?

In principle the broader lesson to draw from this discussion is that one can ask about the social and historical construction of the experiences of any social groups. For example, in later chapters we will encounter the domestication research on teleworkers, single parents and the young elderly

(Haddon and Silverstone, 1993, 1995a, 1996). But how we live these roles and what we expect of them is influenced by wider discourses and representations, by institutional and financial arrangements as well as a range of other factors (including the ICTs available to them). For example, contemporary young elderly can have some different experiences from the young elderly of the 1960s.

Moving back the central focus of the chapter, we saw how parent–child interactions around ICTs were affected by developments in children's mobility and their presence in or absence from different public and private spaces. This provides an example of how new issues can emerge because of changing social trends as well as because of changes in the technology available in the household. Ultimately much of this particular research has focused on the home, although we would have to ask how widespread children's 'media-rich bedroom culture' is within an international context as well as among different subgroups of children. Looking outside the home, there are still questions about variations in the extent to which children participate in various organized activities, and about how they occupy and behave in different public spaces like the street, the shopping mall or in the informal times and spaces within school life. After all, these are all places where they can encounter, experiment with, make sense of and develop collective practices relating to ICTs.

The material on youth and ICTs allows us to look beyond the home and family to make sense of behaviour, or young people's interests, by examining the particularities of their social network. The main focus was on the way the (existing) high degree of peer orientation among this group can shape relations with ICTs. More generally, we see in the example of 'hanging out' using IM as one way in which old practices can find new forms through technologies. While gift relationships can be used as a framework for looking at the interactions of older groups, the various gifting relationships relating to mobile phones are especially useful for making sense of a range of young people's practices. Moreover, in the course of looking at these examples, qualitative research in particular has forced us to look beyond narrow definitions of 'use' (e.g. using the mobile to make certain calls). It is important to reflect on what people do with their technology, when not 'using' it in the narrow sense – i.e. how they interact around the object.

Finally, as we have more and more ICTs, including modes of communication, available to us, we can look holistically at the whole ensemble and ask about the relationships between the different technologies and options. This will be explored more fully in Chapter 9 on careers. But it means that instead of asking why we use a particular technology or mode of communication we can ask why we choose it – given there are alternatives. The use of textual messaging by young people provides a few examples of the type of factors affecting those choices.

Notes

1. There are other themes in the children and ICTs literature, such as questions of identity formation: for example, how children construct their identity as gendered subjects through the use of ICTs (Buckingham, 2002).
2. In this respect, Livingstone (2002) noted some national differences in conceptions of childhood even within the European study, particularly in relation to the degree of autonomy seen as being appropriate for children of different ages.
3. For example, Livingstone (2002) observed that there were not only some similarities between the UK and USA, but also some differences between the UK and Germany. If we look further afield, one Japanese study pointed to the relative smallness of Japanese homes, and the fact that young people rarely had private rooms but often shared a room with a parent or sibling. They rarely met friends at home, since they were worried about offending parents by being too rowdy. Hence, Japanese youth socialized chiefly on the streets, or in spaces 'run by indifferent adults' such as fast-food restaurants, karaoke spots or family restaurants (Ito and Daisuke, 2003). A Korean study also explained that young people do not really have the type of personal space in the home implied in the discussions of bedroom culture (e.g. their rooms are accessible to other family members without permission) (Yoon, 2002).
4. This Israeli study found that 27 per cent of parents were concerned about sexually explicit images on the Internet, 31 per cent about violence depicted there and 46 per cent about online material interfering with their children's values and beliefs: Ribak and Turow (2003), based on a study cited in the workshop on Domesticating the Internet, Commercializing the Family: A Comparative Look at Families, the Internet and Issues of Privacy, University of Haifa, 4–6 June 2001.
5. In the Israeli study, 60 per cent of parents were concerned that some adults would take advantage of their children when online. But this probably reflects a particular high-profile event in that country when one teenager was lured to his death by terrorists through the Internet.
6. Children sometimes want to avoid the embarrassment of inopportune calls from parents. One Finnish study noted how parents' use of texting to check that their children were OK was a less intrusive means of monitoring than by voice (Kasesniemi and Rautianen, 2003).

7. In a longitudinal study by British Telecom, 41 per cent of the children paid the whole bill and just over a third (34 per cent) paid some of the bill. Even for younger teens, financial independence is becoming important. Of course, some parents encourage young people to buy their own prepaid cards as a way of introducing their children to independent financial management.

8. Two-fifths of parents in the USA used filtering software (Lenhart et al., 2001).

9. Apart from relations with parents it is worth adding that there are also institutional constraints on young people's use of the mobile – for example mobiles are banned in some UK and Japanese schools and confiscated if found (Green, 2001; Ito and Daisuke, 2003). This is not just because of the ringing in class but also because they might be stolen (Green, 2001). Of course, in practice youth sometimes resist these controls as well, for example, by making calls on their mobiles in the 'private' spaces within schools (one girl informant in this UK study reported that when she went into the toilets she found a whole group of girls talking on the phone).

10. Instant messaging plays something of a similar role on the Internet (Lenhart et al., 2001).

11. The examples come from Finnish research by Kasesniemi and Rautianen (2002).

12. While not particular to youth, another dimension of gift-giving analysed in French research is in giving out one's mobile phone number to others, and the expectation of reciprocity. Thus exchanging numbers can reflect and become a token of the trust that has been built up between people (Licoppe and Heurtin, 2001).

13. This can happen if the credit on one person's prepayment card is used up, in which case he or she can borrow the phone from other peers. The way in which mobile network charges are organized means that it is sometimes cheaper to use a friend's mobile because he or she is on the same network as the person being called.

14. Similar observations were made in a Japanese study of youth (Ito and Daisuke, 2003). The participants discussed the expectation of receiving a reply within thirty minutes, the criticism they might expect if they were late in replying, and what counted as legitimate reasons for not replying. The researchers argued that this constituted a new kind of discipline on youth, a pressure to be so available to peers, but they also drew attention to the strategies for negotiating non-availability. For example, sending an email about one's intention to take a bath was a 'kind of virtual locking of the door' on peers.

15. The abbreviations and shorthands could also make it difficult to understand the intent of messages, especially if humour or sarcasm was involved (Eldridge and Grinter, 2001).
16. For an extended discussion of the nature of fashion and mobile phones, see Ling (2004).

4

Managing Relationships through and around ICTs

Chapter 3 reminded us how the individual's use of ICTs, in this case that of child and youth, takes place in a wider social context of their relationships with parents and peers. It showed how the use of even personal ICTs could be regulated by others. This influence can be missed in studies that emphasize individual motivations and choices as shaping patterns of behaviour.

Following the main emphasis in British domestication research to date, this chapter starts by more generally looking at the home context in which individuals 'consume' technologies. This is a space where various household members have commitments, routines and general demands on time and space as well as values, hopes and concerns. These all interact and shape that consumption. For example, non-users of ICTs, partners as well as parents, might nevertheless act as 'gatekeepers', influencing the very adoption process and subsequent patterns of usage.

First, we explore what lessons can be learnt from research looking at the tensions around and the regulation of the traditional fixed phone. We will do this mainly by exploring how and why people try to control outgoing and incoming calls. Why is this an issue within households? And what types of control strategies are used? In fact, here we see one of the few attempts to turn the more qualitative orientation of the domestication approach into quantitative measures in order to have some understanding of the scale of these types of household processes.

Apart from parent–child relationships, gender relations in the home have long been identified as a major consideration affecting the experience of ICTs. What has research suggested about those aspects of relationships between males and females in the home that might relate to different gender usage of ICTs such as the Internet? Meanwhile, the telephone literature has pointed to gender divisions of labour in the field of communication, specifically in terms of women's traditional role of managing relationships with the outside world. In which case, one question is whether new modes of communication and new practices accompanying them have any bearing upon this gendered pattern of behaviour.

We turn next to a study of communications with the extended family, partly because much of the discussion of maintaining social networks and providing social support emphasizes the positive role of ICTs in communication. But if we want to approach this with a more critical eye we could ask what conflicts of interests and obligations are involved in maintaining this particular familial social network.

Lastly, the chapter looks at debates on 'sociability' within the home – referring principally to North American discussions. It shifts the focus to the consequences of ICT use, asking specifically whether time spent online detracts from time spent with family members.

Controlling Communication

The mid-1990s British domestication studies provided qualitative evidence of how the cost of telephony was an issue in many households (Haddon, 1994).[1] Norwegian studies have further illustrated the arguments that take place within the home about the phone bill, especially concerning the use of the phone by teenagers (Ling, 1998; Ling and Helmersen, 2000; Ling, 2004). The British qualitative studies suggested that while telephony costs were less of a problem in those relatively more affluent households with few economic worries, it was very much an issue for more than just the poorest in society (Haddon, 1994). For example, many of the middle-class households studied had limited disposable income, since the parents had committed their money to high mortgages or children's private education. Such lifestyle choices meant they still had to be careful about their expenditures, including spending on telephony.

Nevertheless, in those British studies concern about phone costs was most acute among those living on low incomes, namely many of the single parents studied and some elderly people living solely on state benefits. These were the very people for whom the phone could be vital in the event of emergencies or as a social lifeline when they felt trapped in the home in the evenings. Worry about phone bills led to both groups steering outgoing calls to times when cheaper tariffs operated, when possible. Unfortunately ringing up various state agencies and the local council about problems related to living on a low income generally had to be done in the daytime. Calls were also rationed, both in terms of the number of calls and their length. Often, children's use was rationed, with the instigation of rules about what counted as necessary and unnecessary calls. In such households, children obviously had less access to a communications resource than many of their peers and experienced some sense of disadvantage. Despite such measures, the phone bill often remained a source of anxiety, always threatening to spiral out of control.

Large phone bills could sometimes become a very serious concern indeed in the case of communal living arrangements or when families had other people sharing their household, such as lodgers or au pairs. The studies picked up horror stories of huge bills arriving due to illicit use of the phone. Bills could also be an issue between partners, and one that had been exacerbated sometimes by the introduction of itemized billing. More frequently, as in the Norwegian studies, phone bills were a source of heated debate between parents and teenage children, especially concerning the costs relating to the latter's social calls – more so when money was tight.

But it was not just the cost of calls that could be a source of discontent. A French study noting 'the war of the telephone' has already been discussed in Chapter 3 on children (Martin and de Singly, 2000). In addition, where one household member took over the phone, blocking the phone with their frequent or long calls, this denied access to others. Again, the Norwegian studies provided examples where blocking was a source of tension (Ling, 1998).

Incoming calls were problematic for other reasons.[2] In the British studies, participants sometimes made reference to the various unwanted phone calls from acquaintances whom they preferred to avoid. But even apart from these, there were times when people found incoming calls in general to be intrusive upon their peace and privacy. In the light of feminist writings on the way in which women network over the phone, it is worth adding that this was not just a male response to the outside world invading the haven of the home. Women too, especially those who were major users of the phone for work or at work, could suffer from 'phone fatigue'. They wanted a break from the demands of the telephone and sometimes would rather interact with their partners or children. There were periods when incoming calls interfered with the routines of the home, coming at unsociable or simply inconvenient times – such as late at night or early in the morning, or when parents were getting children off to school or nursery or putting them to bed (also discussed in more depth in Lacohée and Anderson, 2001).

The whole issue of the disruptiveness of calls arose most acutely in the study of teleworkers for a variety of reasons. Here there was a frequent assumption on the part of employers or clients that because teleworkers were home-based they could be contacted about work issues outside of normal core working hours – i.e. at evenings and weekends. While this was not deemed to be a problem by some teleworkers, for others it was disruptive to family life. On the other hand, friends sometimes did not appreciate that, even if they were at home, teleworkers still had to get through their workload. Incoming social calls to teleworkers could be a distraction from that work. In addition, the sheer volume of calls into the home often increased with the arrival of telework, meaning that other members of the teleworker's household would occasionally feel pestered by the phone.

Finally, the British studies in general found that other household members could resent the number of calls coming in for someone who was at the heart of large social networks (such as, but not only, teenage children). They could also resent the fact that they had to take on the role of secretary, forever answering calls and taking messages for that person.

The British studies showed how strategies to handle conflicts about outgoing calls entailed both social and technological solutions. Persuasion worked only some of the time. But there were plenty of examples of parents who managed to ration their children's calls, limit them to times when low tariffs operated or succeed in defining 'necessary' and 'unnecessary' communications. Where such persuasion did not work, the issue could remain an ongoing sore point. Or else parents resorted to other strategies such as charging children for telephone use or deducting pocket money to pay for their calls.[3]

Another tactic involved attempting to control the location of the phone. One variation of this involved not allowing children to have access to extensions or cordless phones, and placing the main phone handset in a relatively public place within the home, such as an entrance hall. As we saw in Chapter 3 on children, this meant that calls could be more easily monitored. Alternatively, some of the parents who were studied tried to make the location as uncomfortable as possible. It must be added, though, that determined teenagers appeared to be able to settle down to long phone calls even in the most awkward of spaces. Some parents utilized call-barring, i.e. stopping either incoming or outgoing calls at some points of the day, or allowing only local calls. As an extreme measure, one parent even resorted to sabotaging his teenage daughter's handset.[4]

The five-country Telsoc survey attempted to map in quantitative terms the extent to which these issues existed in households and the extent of efforts to control outgoing communication (Haddon, 1998a).[5] It is worth spending just a little time to look at the detail because this aspect of consumption is only rarely covered in quantitative studies. It underlines, too, the importance of focusing on the household, not just the individual.

The first question in the survey asked whether household members received complaints about their phone calls for a variety of reasons.[6] Here, the existence of complaints was taken to indicate that phone use was an issue. In addition, complaining was in itself a verbal means of trying to influence other people's usage. While only a minority in each country mentioned any specific complaints, these were sizeable minorities ranging from 13 to 32 per cent. The same complaint, about cost, was the most important one in all the countries. In the European sample, females received far more of every complaint compared to males. Meanwhile, a substantial proportion of children, rising to nearly two-thirds of British 14–17 year olds, received complaints about the cost of their phone calls. The finding about children might have been anticipated from the research cited earlier, but the scale is perhaps a little surprising – that so many children across Europe receive complaints.

A second question asked about whether people made an effort to control the use of the phone.[7] In the European sample, nearly two-thirds tried to use cheaper tariffs or else tried to limit their own use. Clearly, while the various national telephone companies are usually interested in encouraging greater use of the phone or related services, a high proportion of consumers are already exercising some restraint upon their usage.

As regards incoming calls, a substantial minority (37 per cent) did find calls to be disruptive. However, there was a wide range in responses to the perception of disruptiveness across the countries. Perhaps this reflects some cultural variation in the extent to which different nationals value a domestic life uninterrupted by the intrusiveness of the outside world. There were questions in the survey about the various strategies that interviewees used to control incoming calls.[8] In contrast to the case of controlling outgoing calls, only a very small proportion of people in all the countries used any of the strategies frequently.

Another strategy for controlling calls was available to those with an answering machine: filtering calls.[9] This is particularly interesting because this application was not the basis upon which the technology had originally been marketed. Filtering calls – checking who calls before deciding whether to answer – involved quite a radical change in practice. The answering machine was sold on the basis that it could take calls when people were out, but it was being used to take them even when they were at home. Generations have learnt to answer the phone when it rang – indeed, many have talked about the psychological difficulty involved in ignoring the ringing phone. Nowadays forms of filtering are more commonplace, e.g. the caller display service enabling one to identify the caller. Indeed, some young people reported sending mobile phone calls to their voice mail immediately they saw on the screen who was calling. But originally filtering by answering machine was not intended by the technology developers, or at least it was not promoted by them. In this sense, the practice of filtering illustrates people's appropriation of a technology, a practice learnt through experimentation, but probably also learnt through informal channels of personal communication (i.e. people telling each other what they have learned to do with the device). In fact, the survey found that by the mid-1990s the practice was widespread. In the European sample, half of the people with answering machines used the devices at some time to filter calls.

Gender Relationships in the Home and ICT Usage

There have been a number of different types of explanation accounting for gender differences in the take-up and use of ICTs. For example, when the first home computers appeared, one explanation of the reluctance of women to use them related to questions of general gender identity. The connotations and symbolism associated with the machine at that time were, it was argued, opposed to constructed notions of femininity (Turkle, 1988). This line of argument about the (mutual) social construction of gender and of technology is one tradition of gender analysis that can be found in various guises (Berg and Aune, 1993; Frissen, 1996, Rommes, 2002). For example, several writers have tried to account for a reoccurring pattern whereby a number of ICTs, including the Internet, were male dominated when they first appeared but later the amount of use by males and females became more even. These writers suggest that when women initially perceived these ICTs as 'technologies' they were less comfortable with them. But when they later redefined ICTs as 'tools' for achieving some purpose in which they were interested, this helped women to feel more at ease (Cockburn and Ormrod, 1993 (on microwave ovens); Singh, 2001; Rommes, 2002 (on the Internet)).

Other hypotheses about gender and adoption of ICTs relate more directly to gender relations specifically within the home, coming closer to some of the interests within the domestication approach. For example, a review of French studies concluded that the appropriation of ICTs by females seemed to be more circumscribed. They had less knowledge of techniques. They mainly used the technologies for functional purposes. And they were reluctant to enter into a dialogue with the machine. The review argued that in order to understand this pattern it was important to examine what was happening in relation to wider gender roles. This included the continued greater involvement of women in domestic labour, which limited the spare time they had available to use ICTs (Jouet, 2000).

We might, in this light of this plea to look at general gender roles, consider an earlier study of the women's relation to the VCR. This argued that women resisted learning to use the device. Women exhibited a 'calculated ignorance', in order to avoid acquiring yet another domestic task – one of setting the video to record programmes for other family members (Gray, 1992). Or to take an example from a later Israeli study of mobile telephony, it was women rather than men who emphasized the importance of being reachable by other household members, reflecting a role of managing the home (Lemish and Cohen, 2003).

A different account, but still one focusing on gender relationships in the home, came from a French study of people learning to use the Internet (Lelong and Thomas, 2001). After a discussion of male monopolization of the Internet, the authors added that women were frequently wary of getting involved in home use, even when they were competent. The women talked about the expertise of the main user (e.g. women said that their male partners knew about the Internet better than them). That expertise was also recognized in the fathers' ability to set rules about children's use, defining what was tolerated, forbidden and what the priorities should be in using the Net. But at the same time other family members had a right to claim certain services from the male expert – to ask him to do something for them online.

In fact, when the Internet first arrived some of the males interviewed had actually been enthusiastic about getting other household members to learn to use it. But this project was usually abandoned. In part this was because female partners showed less interest but it was also because, it often seemed to the researchers, the females did not want to enter into the situation of being a novice in relation to the (male) expert (a process also observed in one of the examples given in a Dutch study by Rommes, 2002). For the authors this was important, in the light of discourses about unequal access, if as a consequence it helped to maintain a gendered division of labour.[10]

Managing Relationships with the Outside World

Some of the earliest empirical analyses of traditional telephony drew attention to the fact that the women make more of the social calls that bind households into social networks (Rakow, 1988; Moyal 1989), a role also observed in later British and French studies (e.g. Lacohée and Anderson, 2001; Mercier, 2001). The latter French study puts this into context by pointing out that women are responsible for maintaining social links in general and do so with letters as well. So this behaviour is not unique to the phone (Mercier, 2001). These studies repeatedly find that, overall, women call more often, for a longer time, take more pleasure in calls and treat the telephone more as a medium for conversation, compared to men, who treat it more as a tool.

That said, a more nuanced picture of how gender patterns change over the life course will be provided in Chapter 8.

So what happens with the arrival of the mobile phone and email – the latter especially through access at work? While many people had always made private calls from the workplace, the French study cited previously found that these technologies led to an increasing number of private communications by males (Mercier, 2001).[11] Some of the quotes from the qualitative interviews also provided examples of people saying that when they had a few minutes free at work they might send a social email. Or if they had a few minutes to spare in the workday (and plenty of 'free' minutes on their mobile that go with the tariff package) they might make a social call on the mobile phone.

Part of the reason for this increase in male social communication was that they simply have more access to the technologies, especially email, through work. As the researcher pointed out, if that were the only factor, would this changing balance of calls between males and females be only transitory? As women also obtained more access to these technologies, would they take back their traditional role as 'ambassadors of the home'?

However, this is not the only factor. Another, Mercier argued, was that while women preferred the transparency of the phone, the way it felt 'natural', men actually took some pleasure in interacting with the technology. Using email required some technical competence. The multiplicity of functions on the mobile differentiated it from the fixed phone. One parallel that comes to mind was the social communications of ham radio users, who enjoyed the very act of achieving communication through using the technology.

The French study described how the characteristics of communications by mobile and email often followed a 'masculine model'. This was due partly, but only partly, to the work contexts in which the calls were made (including the other activities people were involved in when working, the ambience of this space, etc.). Such a context encouraged speed, efficiency and an emphasis on the functionality of the exchange, treating the media as tools rather than as channels for developing a conversation. This form of communication often involved conveying precise information. It rarely entailed making contact just to have a chat.

Given the preceding discussion of gender roles and managing social relationships outside the home, it seems an appropriate moment to add some critical reflections arising from another French study (Segalen, 1999). This qualitative study looked at the contact between three generations, all of whom were adult (indeed, some of the youngest had children themselves). In the study, the generations were called the 'old', the 'pivotals' and the 'young'.

Looking at phone communication between the grandparents and their adult children (the old and the pivitols in this generational chain), usually contact was between mothers and daughters. Given the latter were often working and even had grandchildren of their own, there were many examples when calls were kept short, apart from exceptional circumstances such as sickness and births. Calls were often made to check how the grandparents were getting on, especially if they were alone. Meanwhile the grandparents were often hesitant about calling because they thought it might disturb their children. Nevertheless, they appreciated receiving phone calls, especially if they did not have a large circle of siblings to call. Some of the children (the pivotals) observed that their parents complained that they did not call them enough. The children sometimes resented this demand as being a burden.

Turning to relations between the grandparents and grandchildren (the old and the young), this was often mediated by the pivotals. The grandparents might be in direct contact with certain grandchildren to whom they were particularly close. But some grandchildren once again saw calls to grandparents as a duty and a burden. Sometimes, because of the gap of two generations, some social mobility had taken place and the generations no longer shared the same values or mutual expectations. Some grandparents were so removed from their grandchildren in every sense of the word that they did not understand the behaviour of this age group and sometimes they were annoyed at the degree to which the young people spent time calling friends. Occasionally, the telephone relationship, instead of bringing the generations together, could further poison the rapport between the two sides. Some grandparents preferred to send a card for birthdays rather than call. Some calls from grandchildren to grandparents seemed like formal ritualized acts, devoid of content and emotion. Rather than bringing the generations together, they marked the distance between them.

Lastly, the authors considered relations between the parents and the adult children (the pivotals and the young). Again, much of the contact was between mother and daughter. This was often very positive, preserving independence while maintaining contact. But for some of the young, such contact was again felt to be a duty. Some parents now complained they were not called often enough by their children, whereas the children thought that they did call them enough. In particular, the sons were the ones least likely to call, which sometimes led to more bitterness and complaints. For some children, dealing with the in-laws (pivotals) could also be difficult if the culture of that family was different. Meanwhile, some of the male children, in particular, considered the calls from their mothers to be an interference in their private lives. When they did talk to their mothers, what was for the females 'idle talk' or 'chatter' was perceived as 'twaddle' or 'ramblings' by the males. In other words, telephoning (or its absence) could itself be an object of conflict leading to rancour and bitterness.

Sociability within the Home

There are multilevel, originally North American-based, debates about the effect of Internet use on various forms of social relationships. Many of these relationships are with people outside the home. Hence, this aspect will be covered in Chapter 5 on social networks. But we can take note even at this stage that several different elements, and several different debates or discourses, are at work here. These include debates about whether the Internet increases isolation or leads to more sociability, and the consequences for social well-being and one's quality of life. They cover discussions about sources of social support in daily life, and they deal with issues of civic involvement and participation in society and communities. As well as measuring our links to others beyond the home, the discussions refer to evidence concerning measures of psychological experiences such as loneliness, stress and depression. Among these discussions, albeit with a lower profile in the overall debates, are references to what we might call, for want of a better word, 'sociability within the home'.

This concern about technology's impact on family life actually has a longer history than the Internet. For example, we have the literature claiming that television had led to a decline in family activities (Nie, 2001). We should pause here to draw attention to how this theme reoccurs within other chapters. Chapter 3 on children, we saw the specific concern about the impact of ICT use on children's time for other activities. But that discussion, again, included a package of elements such as children's general sociability (with other children) and their time for creative and imaginative play. Meanwhile, in Chapter 9, on the careers of ICTs, we will look at the issue of time displacement, where the arguments concern how technology is taking time away from other activities in daily life.

What is being considered in this section is specifically time 'for the family' (or for partners). Taking the North American figures, if people are now spending ten to fifteen hours a week online there is the question of where this time is coming from. One approach, backed up by empirical studies, has been to argue that only part of it comes from displacement of other activities. Some of it must come from social time spent with others, including the family (Nie, 2001).[12]

Before the Internet emerged as a mass market, related concerns occurred in discussions of the effects of early computers (e.g. Turkle, 1984, reflecting upon its consequences for teenagers and hackers). These anxieties were picked up in media coverage referring to 'computer addiction' and even to 'computer widows' (i.e. the female partners of very enthusiastic male computer users, who spent a large amount of time at their machines).[13] Worries about the antisocial, solitary nature of Internet use reflected the particular concern about males, especially, devoting more time to their engagement with technologies rather than using that time to develop their social skills.

The first point to make in response to these concerns is that, literally, not all the time interacting with the PC was an isolated activity. The US Homenet study and Israeli research both described the degree of sociability around the PC in the home, noting the various occasions when it can bring families together (Frohlich and Kraut, 2003; Mesch, 2003).

Turning now to the more recent Internet debates, an initial observation is that a range of different measurements appears to be involved here. Sometimes we are looking at self-reports of a decline in sociability (i.e. asking people whether they think there has been a decline after adoption). Some studies compared non-users with users, or users who used the Internet for different amounts of time, looking to see if there were differences in the time they spent with their family. Sometimes we are looking at (relatively small-scale) panel studies, charting the time use of the same people as they move from being non-users to users (Kraut et al., 1998).

If we look more closely at what is being measured, the Homenet study measured 'family communication' in terms of (self reported) minutes spent communicating with family members (Kraut et al., 1998). That research found the greater use of the Internet was associated with a subsequent decline in family communication. In other studies 'time spent with family' was measured (which is obviously slightly different from 'family communication'). In some surveys, Internet use appeared to correlate with less time spent with the family (Nie, 2001; Nie et al., 2002). Yet others found no significant differences in 'family conversation time' (Robinson et al., 2002). A British longitudinal study involving time-use dairies focused on time spent on different activities, including various undertakings in the home. This concluded that there was no evidence that people who now have Internet access were spending less time in 'social' activities in the household (Anderson and Tracey, 2001, 2002). But of course, in itself, measuring these social activities is yet another different measure of sociability in the home.

A second observation about this mixed evidence is that, apart from the range of different measures being employed, there are methodological issues that have been discussed in these debates. For example, there are problems with the self-reporting of time use (Gershuny, 2001; Nie et al., 2002) and because of this, with the reporting of changes in time use. From its qualitative interviews, the British study found that in general, participants found it difficult to answer questions about time displacement and 'even the heaviest users felt that any displacement was marginal at most' (Anderson and Tracey, 2001, p. 264).

Next, as researchers would acknowledge, there is the fundamental problem in estimating change in people's lives (i.e. impacts) from a survey that is made at one point in time (Robinson et al., 2002). This compares different groups of people (e.g. Net and non-Net users). The problem is that they might be different kinds of people in other respects, apart from just being online or not. Internet users might simply have a different social profile from non-users. For example, they might have been less (or perhaps more) sociable within their families in the first place, before they even went online. Therefore, if there were to be an apparent association between Internet use and being less sociable, this would not prove that the first necessarily caused the second. Even in the early Homenet study, the researchers argued that in principle other variables could be at work influencing both family communication and Internet use. One attempt to deal with this problem is via multivariate analysis, to control for other factors such as education, age, marital status, etc. (Nie et al., 2002). The difficulty is that there might still be factors at work that are not anticipated. Some analysts have argued that the only way to avoid this whole problem is by charting changes relating to the same people over time in longitudinal studies (Gershuny, 2001).

A further, emerging, methodological problem may arise as regards measuring time on the Internet. It is one thing to calculate blocks of time when we log on because they show up more clearly in time-use dairies. However, if we move more and more to a situation where the Internet is always on, some Internet use might become more fragmented, as we spend a few seconds or minutes here and there checking things or sending quick messages.

This leads into the question of whether time spent with other people is the (only) appropriate measure of sociability? As in Chapter 2 discussion of how the unevenness of experience of ICTs is measured, should we not be asking about the nature of that experience, rather than just the time involved? Let us take an example to demonstrate a principle. In Chapter 3 on children and ICTs, some of the writers on the social construction of childhood argued that households have become more democratic, less hierarchical and now give more voice to children. In which case, one could argue that even if, hypothetically, time spent on family sociability were to have declined, the experience of the remaining time is nevertheless qualitatively better than when children were 'seen and not heard'. In other words, time itself is not the only consideration if we start to think about the quality of the interactions that constitute sociability.

Finally, while this whole debate shows a concern about potential declining time for family sociability, the latter is not treated in a critical manner. In other words, family sociability is automatically treated as a good thing that we might be losing through technology. The French study discussed in more depth in Chapter 3 on children and ICTs might cause us to reflect just a little upon this (Martin and de Singly, 2000). These researchers looked at (early) teenage use of the phone and in an empirically based typology identified the heaviest phone users as being those whose parents were trying to exert the most parental control of their behaviour. The teenagers were actually using the phone to escape interaction with their parents, to escape 'family sociability', preferring to interact with their friends even if they could not physically be with them (Martin and de Singly, 2000). This example, as well as the others discussed in this chapter, returns us to a theme of the entire book. Family or household interaction is complex and can be viewed from different perspectives. In which case, any evaluation of changes in this interaction needs to reflect this.

Conclusions

Looking at the interpersonal relationships around ICTs, including the tensions and issues that emerge, helps us to understand actual patterns of use. While technologies may have the potential to be used in a variety of ways, we can also start to appreciate the social limitations on that use.

We saw this in the attempts to regulate calls from and to the traditional domestic telephone. But now that the mobile phone and Internet have become more widespread we should ask what effect this has had on strategies aimed at controlling outgoing and incoming communications. How has managing communication become more complex? What bearing have new communications options had on the issues around the home phone that have been described? In what ways have they exacerbated or reduced any tensions? Or, indeed, has the arrival of these communications options raised new issues of control and led to new or ongoing experimentation with strategies for managing communication in everyday life? We will return to some of these questions in Chapter 7 when considering behaviour in public spaces.

While gender is addressed at various points throughout the book, it receives more attention in this chapter, especially in terms of social relationships in the home. If we turn specifically to gender and communications, here at least we are starting to see research considering the consequences of mobile phone and email for managing relationships with the outside world. This asks whether gender roles might be changing. Once again we see the tensions involved in interpersonal relations in the study of communication with the extended family. This suggests complex gender relations – for example, when even the communication between mothers and daughters can be problematic. To what extent and in what ways, if at all, has the spread of the mobile phone and Internet had any bearing upon some of these particular communications?

Lastly, we saw the question about the social consequences of the Internet: whether it has affected sociability within the home, whether time spent online has detracted from time spent with family members. It is not that new a concern. Antecedents existed in the fears voiced in relation to the television and computer. Clearly there are a host of methodological issues behind these debates. But in addition, the whole issue of family sociability needs also to be treated with a more critical eye. This fits in with the attention that has been given to interpersonal tensions as one key theme of this chapter.

Notes

1. This paper was based on the study of teleworkers and single parents, reported in Chapters 2 and 8.
2. Although this chapter is primarily about the traditional fixed-line phone, it is worth adding that the issue of controlling (potential incoming) communication emerges in relation to the mobile phone. For example, many people selectively give out their mobile numbers, but they sometimes decide not to carry the mobile or they manage calls by switching them to voice mail (Licoppe and Heurtin, 2001).
3. In one case, exasperated parents ended up installing a second line for their children, and made them pay for all the calls. The result was that disagreements over bills then took place among the children rather than between the parents and children.
4. One parent got so frustrated that he disabled his daughter's handset so that she could not make outgoing calls from her bedroom. However, she managed to sometimes evade that control by initiating calls on the main phone and then switching them to her bedroom phone to continue her conversation there at leisure.
5. While the original chapter reporting this is in Italian (in Fortunati, 1998), the English version is available at http://members.aol.com/leshaddon/Date.html.
6. The four separate questions concerned whether people received complaints (a) because of the cost of their calls, (b) because they made

or received too many calls, (c) because they blocked the line and (d) because they made too many unnecessary calls.

7. The three questions asked were (a) whether interviewees made their own calls at the times when cheaper tariffs operated, (b) if they limited their own use and (c) if they tried to persuade other people in the household to limit their calls.

8. These were (a) blocking incoming communication in some way (e.g. by leaving the phone off its resting place ('off the hook') so that the call could not arrive, turning the ringer off etc.), (b) not answering calls, (c) getting someone else to answer calls and (d) asking people who phoned into the home to avoid calling at certain times.

9. This involved hearing who was calling before deciding whether or not to answer or instead let the caller leave a message (also discussed in Lacohée and Anderson, 2001).

10. A related point was raised in a Dutch study by Rommes (2003). In this qualitative study, women who attended an Internet course had tried learning from their partners but it had not worked out – hence they went on the formal course instead.

11. Plant (2002) also argues that males were making more social calls now because of the mobile phone.

12. But other US studies find contradicting results. In one, 88 per cent said the Internet had little impact on time with family (or friends) (Katz et al., 2001). In another, more than half of Internet users actually reported more communication with family after going online (Howard et al., 2001). In yet another, 92 per cent of users said that they spent the same amount of time together with household members as before (UCLA, 2000).

13. In fact, one British study looked specifically at this issue in response to these media claims. The findings might lead us to reflect on current debates about the Internet, especially when they concern heavier users of the Internet. Basically, people who developed intense relationships to ICTs such as the computer were likely to have had equally intense involvement in other activities before the PC arrived in their life (Shotton, 1989). The heavy users of this study had not actually changed their patterns of sociability. They had switched from old interests and hobbies to being computer enthusiasts. Moreover, their partners had already known that they had this orientation when they had first formed a couple.

5

Social Networks and ICTs

Just as it was important to look beyond the individual in order to appreciate the influence of other household members, so it is important to consider the general influence of wider social networks, as we did more specifically in the case of youth peers. This provides another context for understanding an individual's actions, choices and experience of ICTs.

We start by asking in what different ways social networks have a bearing upon people's interest in and appreciation of ICTs. When do social networks actually supply the ICTs that enter people's homes? In what different ways do they then support actual usage? Next, the chapter considers extending the domestication framework beyond the home, asking what we would need to know to appreciate the processes by which ICTs are 'domesticated' by social networks.

The remainder of the chapter makes a link to North American debates seen in Chapter 4 on the social consequences of ICT. But now it examines concerns about the effects of the Internet on people's relationships with their social networks. Part of that discussion related to concerns about the solitary nature of Internet use. So first we must once again ask whether such use is always solitary or indeed asocial. In this respect, what can we learn from such claims about previous ICT use – especially computer use? And then what do the balance of findings now suggest about the influence of Internet use on people's relation with their social networks, taking into account some issues around the method and measurements involved?

The other part of this debate concerns the question of whether the communications options enabled by the Internet leads to online communication displacing offline communication. Is such a displacement actually occurring? How should we evaluate the quality of online compared to offline communications and its role in our lives? This in turn leads to further questions. To what extent do people build strong relationships through online contact? Does this lead to offline contact? To what extent does communication via the Internet help to sustain social networks? What types of relationships does it help to maintain or support? Lastly, by way of contrast, does mobile phone communication suggest a very different outcome from the Internet debate? Might the very weak ties that exist with the strangers around us diminish further because of the mobile?

Social Networks Supporting ICT Acquisition and Use

Social networks can provide one route through which we acquire ICTs. Such networks provide a means by which information about technologies and services can be disseminated. They can actually stimulate interest, as when people mention that they do not want to be left behind by their other network members. British research observed that if some people in social networks own a technology, this increases the likelihood of other people in the same network owning that technology (Tracey, 1999).

Social networks can enable people to gain familiarity with technologies. One European five-country qualitative study of the Internet showed that even many non-users had actually tried out the Net or had seen it in action at the homes of friends and family (Haddon, 1999a).[1] Some non-users had even asked people in their social network to look up things for them online and through this process they came to appreciate the Web's usefulness. A Canadian qualitative study drawing attention to the same processes referred to the role of the 'warm expert' in many people's stories about how they acquired ICTs. These warm experts were friends or relatives who had relatively more expertise than the people interviewed, but who were also close to them and willing to help a novice (Bakardjieva, 2001).

However, the opposite side of the coin is where social networks are not able to support interest. Some people in the European study moved in social circles whose members were not interested in or familiar with the Internet. For example, sometimes their work colleagues were not required to use the Internet for work. Or else they had retired and many of the people of their generation were not familiar with the online world. As a result, even if they showed some interest themselves it was difficult for them to know where to start. There was no one to turn to for help (Haddon, 1998c).

Social networks influence ICT adoption in yet other ways. People acquire ICTs from members of their networks (Bakardjieva, 2001). This is perhaps especially true of relatives, and more so of close family. British studies from the early 1990s pointed to the small gifts that people can receive from relatives, such as phone handsets (Haddon, 2000b). A number of the young elderly studied had acquired more expensive ICTs, such as VCRs, as presents from their adult children (Haddon and Silverstone, 1996). Later research made similar observations about mobile phones and even computers (for example, when someone in the extended family upgraded and passed on the old machine). Sometimes the recipients would not have considered getting ICTs if they had not received them as gifts (Tracey, 1999).

After acquisition, social networks can continue to support the use of ICTs. For example, numerous studies have indicated how members of social networks can provide practical support, such as helping to set up equipment and software or solve technical problems (Haddon, 1999a; Tracey, 1999; Bakardjieva, 2001; Lelong and Beaudouin, 2001). In fact, in British research even some teleworkers mentioned that their social networks were important in this respect. Their workplace-based technical support staff could not always support employees who worked at home (Haddon and Silverstone, 1993).[2] Once again, if this expertise does not exist in a particular person's social networks, such technical difficulties can be difficult to overcome.

Apart from supporting usage, social networks can also influence the form it takes (Tracey, 1999). We saw this in Chapter 3 on children and youth. Young people's perceptions of what counted as interesting websites to visit could be influenced by their peers. As one analyst put it, the social network members who help people to learn about the Internet are passing on what they had discovered, including 'their definitions of the new technology crystallised from their own experience' (Bakardjieva, 2001, p. 7).

If we turn specifically to the case of telecoms, the European P-903 study showed that the structure of social networks could influence usage in the sense of having a bearing upon their members' communication patterns (Smoreda and Thomas, 2001).[3] Meanwhile, the five–country qualitative study of the Internet found that lack of access to certain social networks could be restrictive. If one is the only person accessing the Net within one's social networks then this can limit the range of use since there is no one to act as a guide to the types of things that can be achieved online (Haddon, 1999a).

Researchers have tried to differentiate further the influences within social networks, rather than just talk about the role of social networks in general. To give a flavour of this type of analysis, some have looked at the different influence of friends versus family or the special relations between adult children and their parents. Sometimes overlapping with this, other analysts have focused on strong and weak ties, with one review arguing how weak ties – meaning the members of one's network who are not close, such as acquaintances – were useful for providing access to new resources and ideas (Tracey, 1999). Looking at communications patterns, yet other researchers have explored contact with local versus distant social network members, changes in social networks over the life course (such as teenagers' and young adults' larger circles of friends) and the impact of residential relocation on social networks (Smoreda and Thomas, 2001).

Finally, it is worth observing that many of the approaches to analysing social networks that have been outlined above stress how individuals and households are influenced by their networks. Looked at another way, the implication is that individuals and households support their own social network's experience of ICTs. Some of their own usage is on behalf of friends, relatives etc. More generally, giving support, advising and showing their expertise within these social networks itself constitutes part of people's very experience of these technologies.

The Domestication of ICTs in Social Networks

To illustrate the process of how ICTs found a role within social networks of peers, we will consider the history of the first home computers in the UK during the early 1980s. Part of their appeal, leading to a boom in 1983, was fuelled by the futurologists, politicians, technology enthusiasts and media analysts who portrayed these machines as an icon of the coming IT revolution. Many people purchased these early computers because they were concerned not to be passed by. Parents certainly did not want their children to miss out (Haddon and Skinner, 1991). But one then has to make sense of the fact that for many years the main use of these machines was actually for playing games. Even suppliers were concerned about the extent to which those devices were becoming just games machines.[4]

Electronic games first appeared in public arcades and were originally adopted by some arcade owners as replacements for pinball. It was here that (some) male youth collectively developed the culture of game-playing, competing to get high scores, learning tricks and strategies from others and swapping tips. When home games machines appeared and later when home computers became a platform for playing games, this culture continued. For example, interviews with British youth revealed that many of the boys who were playing games in the 1980s played at times in isolation. But they also talked about games at school. They swapped games. They compared notes as regards tactics. And they passed on the information about ways to cheat or get around games problems – information that was starting to appear in game magazines. By contrast, while girls may have played games, on the whole these other layers of interaction were absent among their social networks. Games were not the same topic of conversation as they were for boys. The general reason for looking at such game- and computer-related interactions and practices is that they help explain gender differences in the popularity of games and home computers at that time (Haddon, 1992). For the purposes of this section, it underlines the importance of considering the experience of consumption and relationships outside the home that was first discussed in Chapter 3 on youth.

Later research on mobile telephony among youth, reported in Chapter 3, has also emphasized the importance of peers as contributing to the popularity of the mobile among this group. It drew attention to collective, mobile phone-related practices that were in many ways the equivalent of the computer-related ones outlined above. Sometimes, particular subcultures within youth played a major role in creating interest in ICTs. For example, Japanese researchers reported how the 'Kogyaru', street-savvy high school students, 'in the early nineties and then with mobile phones in the later half of the nineties pioneered and popularised recreational uses of mobile communication, first with pagers' (Ito and Daisuke, 2003).

If one wants to extend the domestication framework to ask how social processes among networks help shape the consumption of ICTs, there are some immediate challenges. Friendship ties, or the sometimes looser relations between young people, are very different from the relationship between family members. Friendship networks are usually not so bounded, as it is not always clear who is part of a group. While the relationships involved can be intense, they are often much weaker than family ones. They have a shorter history and are in many cases more temporary, without the depth that comes when people's biographies are so intertwined as in the case of the family. They do not occur in the same, shared space of a home, although they may involve the colonization of certain public spaces, and they do not entail the equivalent financial relationships that exist in families. On the other hand, as in families, these relationships do have some shared histories and to varying degrees elements of shared identities. They have their own politics and understandings of what is appropriate, and they involve the use of strategies for managing relationships vis-à-vis peers.

Bearing this in mind, we can at least pose the question of how ICTs such as mobile phones are domesticated within such social networks. At this stage, without the longitudinal study of such change, we can only ask questions. For example, what are the processes by which ICTs acquire meaning within such groups (over and above the marketing of firms)? What, for example, leads mobiles or particular mobiles to become fashionable (or not)? What forms of negotiation take place within social networks and how do collective practices emerge? Are there rules about use and if so how are they policed? What type of subsequent career do mobiles have within a group context? In other words the general types of question one would pose within a domestication framework can be applied when trying to investigate how social networks network come to consume ICTs.

The Internet's Effects on Sociability in Social Networks

There are two concerns about the possible negative effects of the Internet on social networks:

1. As a solitary activity, time spent interacting with the Internet may detract from time spent socializing with others.
2. People may use the communication facilities of the Internet to socialize with others online at the cost of the time they would otherwise spend interacting with those whom they normally see face-to-face (and speak to by phone). Part of this concern is related to fears that the quality of those online interactions and relationships are not as good as offline ones.

This section will deal with the first of these arguments, but it will become clearer why it is important to mention the second from the start. We will start with some observations about asocial Internet use, then briefly review some evidence and reflect on the methodological issues.

Chapter 4 touched on a number of reasons why we should be a little wary of assuming that computer or Internet use is always an antisocial activity. In Chapter 3 on children and youth, the fact that young people interacted with each other in media-rich bedrooms showed this. Canadian and British studies have also discussed young people's sociability in front of the screen when online (Millerand et al., 1999; Livingstone, 2001). We can develop the point further by adding that even time spent alone in front of the screen can have a bearing upon time spent socializing later on. If we go back to the early British study of the home computer, we saw a whole range of computer-related activities at school and in other venues outside the home. In relation to the Internet, we saw how it was peers who shaped values about what counts as good sites and shared information about these. Admittedly, both of these arguments relate specifically to young people. Yet, these observations about social dimensions relating to time spent online still need to be made.

When we now look at contemporary Internet studies, what we at first find is conflicting evidence. For example, one US survey reported that heavier Internet use leads to decreased time with (family and) friends (Nie, 2001). Another much publicized piece of research, the Homenet study, initially reported that Internet use led to a decline in local social networks and greater loneliness (Kraut et al., 1998), although a follow-up study of this same group showed that this general effect later disappeared (Kiesler et al., 2000; Kraut et al., 2002).[5]

In contrast, and stressing the sociability benefits of the Internet, we find studies citing evidence that Internet use actually led to increased communication with local friends (e.g. Howard et al., 2001; Kavanaugh and Patterson, 2001).[6] Alternatively, we find responses to particular survey questions which suggested that Internet use actually had little impact on time spent with friends (Katz et al., 2001). They neither increased nor decreased contact with people either in person or by phone (Wellman et al., 2001). In a review that goes far beyond the space that can be allocated to the subject in this book, the authors argued that on balance it looks as if the Internet expanded the interactions with our social networks (Katz and Rice, 2002b)

As regards the methodologies of Internet studies, the issues are the same as in Chapter 4 on sociability within the family, given that the same studies often consider both friends and family. Therefore, we find discussions of the best measures (Nie, 2001), arguments that not all the studies use representative samples (pointed out in Katz et al., 2001) and doubts about using data from self-reports (Kraut et al., 1998). Given that they actually attempt to measure change in behaviour over time, most surveys use cross-sectional and not longitudinal data, opening the door for the potential problem discussed earlier. There might be an association between variables but causality is harder to prove. We might add that, understandably, many measures of the phenomena being studied are possible. One study alone measured how many times people met friends last week, the time spent with friends and the time spent going out socially (Katz et al., 2001). One dilemma, as in the case of the digital divide, is that one can appreciate the scope for conflicting, or at least non-comparable, evidence. On the other hand, approaching the issue with a range of different measures can provide a more nuanced picture of what is a complex issue.

The situation is also made more complicated by some mismatch between certain arguments and evidence. As these debates sometimes acknowledge, the Internet consists of more than one element. One crude division is between those parts that have been characterized as 'interpersonal' (e.g. email, chat) and those characterized as 'informational' (e.g. the things one can do on the Web) (Kraut et al., 2003).[7] Whenever the above studies measure Internet users (as opposed to non-users) or the amount of time spent on the Internet overall, they effectively package together the interpersonal and informational uses, just measuring 'use'. This is despite the fact that at the start of this section we saw that one concern (the Internet can make us more antisocial) is really about informational uses while the other concern (that communicating with distant others detracts from local interaction) focuses on that interpersonal use of the Internet.

The Balance of Offline and Online Interaction

One review of some of the consequences of the Internet for social networks summarized the pessimistic perspective that 'online activity replaces strong social ties in the unmediated world with weak online ties' (Rice, 2002, p. 117). The first point we might address is whether this replacement is actually occurring. An 'online tie' appears to refer to people we do not meet with offline. While the statement itself does not necessarily claim that online interaction is with distant others, there seems to be an assumption that this probably is the case in many of the arguments reviewed.

As a starting point, we might look at the research on telephony, space and communication. Let us take basic voice telephony, which like the Internet has the technological potential to connect us globally. Most fixed-line phone calls are actually local and most phone calls are to people we already see on a regular face-to-face basis.[8] For example, one French study showed how proximity and personal contact could lead to more phone calls. In other words, we do not resort to the phone chiefly because distance makes it difficult to meet people (Smoreda and Licoppe, 1999).[9] Most phone calls not only help to organize face-to-face meetings but also supplement them – we phone people more whom we see, as reflected in patterns of local telephone traffic.[10]

To an extent, the same appears to be true of Internet interaction. British quantitative and qualitative studies of the Internet would reinforce that emphasis on the importance of proximity and of contacting people we already interact with offline. Adults often use email (and chat) to supplement face-to-face meetings, contacting 'local' friends,[11] not only for organizing meetings but also in terms of gift-giving, sending little messages to people to indicate that they are still thought about during the time between meetings (Haddon, 2000c).[12] A review of studies of children's use of the Internet finds similar results about the dominance of online contact with peers who are already known (Livingstone, 2001, 2003).

In such cases, using one medium of communication as opposed to another is not always an either-or choice. One does not simply displace the other. Both are increasingly part of a larger communications repertoire, and many people choose from this repertoire to suit the circumstances,[13] albeit with constraints sometimes operating on those choices (Haddon, 2003a).

Subsequent international empirical research would appear to confirm this, noting, in fact, positive correlations between face-to-face contact, telephone contact and email contact (Chen et al., 2002).

But even when these communications are with those who are at a distance, many calls and messages are still to people whom we know offline first and in some cases with people who we will meet occasionally, such as relatives (discussed later in this chapter). For example, the qualitative component of the European P-903 study showed how the Internet appeared to facilitate contacts with all kinds of people one already knew – kin, friends and acquaintances (Mante-Meijer et al., 2001) – and this was reflected in a whole range of other studies, showing that 'Internet communication complements real-world relations' (Rice, 2002, p. 118).

Lastly, contacts that start online do not always remain so. True, many do. In this respect a variety of studies have observed that some encounters online are short term and primarily 'forms of mutual entertainment' (Miller and Slater, 2000). Yet people can also form strong social bonds online and this can lead to offline contact (Haddon, 2000c, using British qualitative study; Miller and Slater, 2000, based on qualitative research in Trinidad; Kraut et al., 2002, using US survey data; Rice, 2002 and Katz and Rice, 2002, both reviewing further studies; Kanayama, 2003, based on a qualitative study in Japan).

While online communication can lead to such offline contact, there still remains a question of how significant it is. That partly depends on how you evaluate the evidence. One review of US surveys commented that 'over 10% of those who indicated they had met someone on-line went on to meet them in person and the vast majority (85%) indicated that it was a positive experience' (Katz and Rice, 2002b, p. 327). But others have pointed out that developing strong relationships online is comparatively rare (Kraut et al., 2002). This means that even if, in a minority of cases, online contact leads to offline contact, one can at least pose the question of how meaningful and deep a relationship this is.

The Quality of Online Communication

The other part of the concern outlined earlier is about 'weak' online ties. This is the view that the quality of online interactions and relationships is less than that of offline ones. One review of research indicated how this assessment of the inferior quality of computer-mediated communication has been an assumption not only in social psychological research but also in more popular discourses. The evaluation is largely because of claims about the limited 'bandwidth' of textual communication and the anonymity of the media (Watt et al., 2002). The reviewers observed that an equivalent critique of the quality of the medium was also made about new media in the past, such as the telephone.

If we take a particular example of evidence cited in this debate, US researchers reviewed a number of quantitative studies – of business people, of students, of Homenet trial participants' relations with social networks and of those participating in online communities. They compared how these groups evaluated online and offline relationships (Cummings et al., 2002). The conclusion was that computer-mediated communication, and in particular email, was less valuable than face-to-face contact and the telephone for building and sustaining close social relationships. In particular, from looking at listservs on the Internet, the researchers concluded that some of the online communities studied in earlier Internet research, which seemed to be very active, might well have been interesting cases. But they seemed to be the exceptions rather than the rule.

Perhaps, though, we need to develop a more complex assessment of this issue of quality. The Trinidad study described examples where there was surprisingly rich banter online and the researchers were impressed by just what emotions could be expressed through text (Miller and Slater, 2000). A Japanese study of an elderly online community made a similar point, observing that the participants were used to text-based communication. They could express emotion through the use of such devices as archaic language styles, dialect and poetry (Kanayama, 2003). Two reviews of a range of studies also pointed out how online communication could be made very personal and socially rich. In fact, it might not be any less personal or 'real' than face-to-face communication (Rice, 2002; Watt et al., 2002).

A different way of approaching this issue would be to note that the emotional closeness of online contacts might not be what is important for some purposes. We might consider here communication with communities of interest, where weak ties may nevertheless be meaningful. Indeed, it can be quite important simply to know that there are others out there in similar circumstances, for example, facing a particular health problem, and that they can share experiences (Bakardjieva and Smith, 2001).

Finally, when we start to consider contact with people we already know, online communication may be good enough to help maintain relationships. For example, a number of the American studies found that using the Internet increased contact with distant friends and relatives (Kraut et al., 1998; Boneva et al., 2001; Howard et al., 2001; see also an AOL survey reported in Rice, 2002). In one piece of research nearly a third of interviewees (31 per cent) said that they now had more communication with family members whom they previously did not contact often (Howard et al., 2001).[14] The Trinidad study also reported that the Internet led to more contact with such distant relatives (Miller and Slater, 2000). In particular, online communication could take on even more significance for migrants and diaspora. The Trinidadians living abroad used it to stay in touch and the researchers pointed in particular to the role of email for 'reactivating family ties that had fallen into abeyance' (Miller and Slater, 2000, p. 56). Meanwhile, a Canadian study looking at the motivations for going online described how email and online chat were seen as practical ways to restore and maintain contact with family abroad (Bakardjieva and Smith, 2001).

Looking beyond relatives, British qualitative studies showed how email enabled people to maintain contact with other socially distant parts of the network when that might otherwise have been lost. Email has even been used to resurrect contact with previous social networks, such as old school friends (Haddon, 2000c).[15] In one AOL survey, 41 per cent of participants reported that they had renewed such contacts (Rice, 2002). Meanwhile, one Canadian study found evidence that when people move house to a new area, former neighbours living some distance away can still use the Internet to provide online social support (Hampton and Wellman, 2001).

The Mobile Phone and Patterns of Sociability

Various writers have drawn attention to the psychological withdrawal of mobile phone users from the immediate physical social space and those co-present through a preference to interact with spatially 'distant' others (Fortunati, 1997). In some respects this takes us in a different direction from claims about the effects of the Internet on sociability. Like the traditional fixed-line phone, the mobile phone often gives us more contact with people who are socially close to us, who we may well see regularly, and who are net-work members with whom we have strong ties. This can be seen in patterns of mobile phone traffic and was also found in a study of Japanese web-phone use (a mobile phone capable of Internet access and sending email), where email communications were once again sent to well-known persons (Miyata et al., 2003).

This type of communication is indeed sociable. Norwegian research has argued how such intensive communications where 'one has a running sense of the other's location and situation' can reinforce such social ties (Ling, 2004). But it is a certain kind of sociability that excludes other forms. The author referred to the notion of a 'walled community' to convey the idea that when communication is increasingly aimed at a limited number of people we know well, this limits our opportunity to 'establish new ties in one's co-located situation'. As French researchers arguing in a somewhat similar vein have pointed out, since people's attention is limited, this shift in the balance to a more 'connected' relationship with an intimate few can be at the expense of making the effort to interact with strangers (Rivère and Licoppe, 2003). Both the French and Norwegian research drew upon the work of Sennett (1986), describing the growing incivility within society. This leads to the question of whether such a process of interacting with a few close others detracts from the public sphere itself and from the social capital of society (Ling, 2004).

Conclusions

This chapter started by indicating the various ways in which social networks can have a bearing upon people's experience of ICTs. They do this through stimulating initial interest, through providing a way to become familiar with technologies and services as well as appreciating their usefulness, through recommendations and gifts and through assisting and shaping usage. However, if social network support can be a resource, lacking the networks that perform these roles can itself contribute to the unevenness of experience discussed at the start of this book.

The next step was to make the network itself the focus of attention, rather than the individual or household within it, just as some general studies of social networks do. Then we can ask how social networks as collectivities adopt ICTs, and how practices relating to these technologies emerge. In other words, we could extend the domestication framework by asking about domestication by groups other than the household. We saw this demonstrated on a large scale with the example of gender and games, looking even beyond more narrowly defined networks of people who know each other. This illustrated the point that it was sometimes important to look at relations outside the home in order to explain some social phenomenon. In this instance, it helped to account for gender differences in the early usage of home computers arising from the different meaning that games had in networks of boys and girls.

The final section looked at the specific debates about the effects of the Internet on our relationships with social networks, which stressed the potential displacement of some interactions by others. The first concern was that the Internet might reduce people's sociability by cutting down the time they spent interacting with their social networks. This raises some by now familiar methodological debates, to which we might add that to measure simply 'use' of the Internet or time spent interacting with the screen may be misleading. Using the Internet (or other ICTs such as the computer) may not always be as antisocial as is portrayed. Teenagers could be sociable in terms of interacting in front of the screen as well as talking about the Internet when not online.

The second concern is that the Internet could lead to people spending more time interacting with distant others to the detriment of face-to-face contact, couched in terms of weak mediated online ties displacing strong offline ones. Again, there is a question about how fruitful it is to pose the question in this way. Much Internet-based communication is actually with people we already know. The medium has become just one more channel in our overall communications repertoire, used alongside other channels. Moreover, it is questionable whether we should simply talk about 'weak' mediated online ties. The picture is more complex. Whatever its 'quality', communicating online can be useful for some purposes and it can exhibit a richness in certain circumstances.

Notes

1. This study took place in 1998 in Germany, Italy, the Netherlands, Norway and the UK. Commissioned by NCR, it involved twenty in-depth household interviews in each country.
2. As in the case of the single parent and young elderly studies, this research from 1992–3 involved dairies and two sets of interviews with twenty households. The report is available at http://members.aol.com/leshaddon/Date.html.
3. Communication patterns included use of the fixed phone, email and the mobile. These were related to network features such as social network size, the percentage of family versus friends and the percentage of local network members.
4. By way of clarification, most UK computers sold at that time were cheaper and had less capacity and functional capability than computers being sold in North America. This history of computers and games is based on my doctorate research 1984–8, involving the use of secondary sources to construct history of computers and games, and interviews with people working in the British computer and game industry, as well as interviews with users, including young people, and observational studies. The work was supplemented by contemporary survey evidence. The doctorate can be accessed through http://members.aol.co.,Index. html, the history of home computers appears in Haddon (1988a), their use by youth appears in Haddon (1992), and the history of games appears in Haddon (1988b, 1993, 1999c).

5. The authors argue a number of processes may be at work here. One refers to the specific nature of the early sample – the results may have been different for different groups. Another process may be that it has one effect in the short term but another in the longer term. A third is that the first findings may have been influenced by the nature of the Internet at that time. Fewer family and friends were online in 1995–6 compared to the time of the follow-up study in 1998. They also conducted a second panel study to demonstrate differential effects for different groups. Extraverts and those with more social support benefited more from Internet access, including in terms of enhancing relationships with their social networks.

6. European data from the P-903 project would match this. Internet users have larger social networks than non-users and long-term users report more frequent sociability with friends (Smoreda and Thomas, 2001). The British Telecom longitudinal study also found a small increase in social life following take-up of the Internet (Gershuny, 2001).

7. The authors themselves are critical of aggregating Internet data and acknowledge the crudity of this division between interpersonal and informational in order to make a general point.

8. This point was also true historically, as Fischer (1992) pointed out in his American study when reflecting on concerns that the phone favours non-local communication over local communication.

9. Wellman (1992), in his Canadian study, also observed that his respondents had more frequent contact with those who lived nearby – both face-to-face and by telephone.

10. In fact, the P-903 data reinforced the results of other studies showing that the more you see people, the more you call them (Smoreda and Thomas, 2001).

11. That acknowledged, one first caveat is that the term 'local' could have misleading connotations, sometimes implying 'in the neighbourhood'. In 1992 one Canadian study demonstrated that most friends do not live 'locally' in that sense and emphasized how little face-to-face contact there is now with neighbourhood social networks (Wellman, 1992). There is an argument that the 'communities' in which we operate (socially, as opposed to spatially, defined) are more spatially dispersed (Wellman et al., 2001). If the main interest is in social relations in which there is regular face-to-face contact, these can be maintained over a fairly wide geographic area, for example a large city, depending on the area over which people operate in their daily lives. Some people operate only over a relatively small, contained area while others regularly travel over an area the size of London (as in meeting friends

'up in town'). This has to be borne in mind in discussions of 'local' communication.

12. Also observed in the five-country qualitative study of the Internet (Haddon, 1999a) and in a Belgian study of young adults (Hartmann, 2003).

13. Others have commented on how we can move between different modes as our relationships with people evolve (Ling, 2000).

14. A similar figure (2 per cent) was found in the Pew Survey in 2002 (Horrigan et al., 2002a).

15. One of the striking observations about proximity that emerges from that qualitative material is how often interviewees referred to their use of email to keep contact with social network members who lived abroad. This sometimes replaced phone calls, but it also led to additional communications that arose because of the existence of the new medium.

6

Time and ICTs

Our longer-term social commitments, as well as the wider social structures in which we operate, have a bearing upon adoption and use. In this respect temporal constraints, which have consistently received attention in British domestication studies, are important because they have a bearing for people's room for manoeuvre when making decisions about ICTs.

This chapter starts specifically with the following question. How does the time we reserve for other activities limit or shape the consumption of ICTs? Specifically, when can time considerations influence the very adoption of ICTs? In what ways do they limit usage, indeed constrain our ability to learn to use ICTs in the first place? In answering these questions, what type of time considerations should we examine over and above the total amount of free disposable time available to us?

The next section deals with subjective perceptions of time, since these may influence the strategies that people adopt when organizing their time and their attitudes to and use of new ICTs. Here we ask how researchers on 'time stress' have approached and tried to make sense of this issue of time perceptions. How has their analysis contributed to how we might think about the 'quality' of time?

Finally, we return to the social consequences of ICT use, dealing specifically with effects of ICTs on how we plan and manage time. After some general observations about our lack of knowledge of people's time strategies, this section provides some case studies that deal with the degree to which we need to organize time in advance. This leads to the following questions. To what extent, and for whom do ICTs enable more spontaneity or alternatively create the need for the greater pre-planning of time?

Time Influencing the Adoption and Use of ICTs

Disposable Time

If we start with a concept from economics, people sometimes anticipate the 'opportunity costs' of using ICTs – i.e. they recognize that they could be partaking in another activity instead. Anticipation of time costs can affect not only the decision to use ICTs but also the very decision to adopt them in the first place or to invest in the skills necessary to use the technology. This was captured in some comments from the European P-903 study, when people were expressing their reservations about the Internet (Klamer et al., 2000). One complained: 'It takes time to develop into an experienced searcher'. Another added: 'If one isn't selective and doesn't know what one's looking for, surfing, information search and shopping may take too long ... and consume disposable time.'

This whole issue of disposable time is important because the extent that we reserve time for activities in turn imposes potential limits on the consumption of ICTs. We can demonstrate this with an example from the five-country qualitative study of Internet adopters and non-adopters (Haddon, 1999a).[1] For many of the adults interviewed, the time slot when they went online was often restricted by working hours, thus occurring in the evenings or at weekends. Even some teleworkers followed this pattern. For example, one British interviewee allowed herself only thirty minutes to relax and search for whatever interested her on the Internet. This took place in the time slot after she had completed her day's work and before she went out socializing in the evening. For others the time slot might fall after completing some work-related tasks at home in the early evening, or in the late evening, relaxing at the end of the day (e.g. through socializing online). In other words, while some had unpredictable periods of free time, others had more regular time slots for going online.

Occasionally those involved in the Internet industry ask whether the time people actively spend online might increase substantially. One can imagine how it might increase somewhat, and how the pattern of use might change to frequent short bursts of activity with the 'always on' Internet. But, in the short term at least, how substantially can Internet time increase for people such as the interviewees described above if the Net competes against their commitments to and desire to be with family, with friends and to take part in other activities inside and outside the home?

The Timing of ICT Use

A number of ICTs are promoted not so much for saving time as for being able to time-shift activities. Examples would be VCRs, answering machines and voice mail. Or else these technologies offer temporal flexibility in that people can use them when they want to. This includes communicating with people at the timing of one's own choice, without being constrained by fixed time schedules or the pressure to reply to communications immediately. Examples would include Video-On-Demand, remote banking and shopping, and (answering) asynchronous communication media such as emails and text messages. Of course, by offering users more flexibility in organizing their lives, this may in turn allow them to combine activities in such a way so as to save time.

That is the technological promise. Certainly participants in the European P-903 project realized this to some extent (Klamer et al., 2000). However, our ability to shift time is also constrained by the social structures in which we live, even if we acknowledge that some people have more flexible temporal patterns than others. French analysts studying phone communication patterns found that the overall distribution of phone calls was still shaped by patterns of work, when shops were open and when transport and other public services operated. To an extent this remains so even as there are moves towards twenty-four-hour, seven-day-a-week working and opening hours. Influenced by the timing of work and of school, French domestic calls start to rise at 5.00 p.m. peaking at 8.00–9.00 p.m. (De Gournay and Smoreda, 2001).[2]

Then there is the question of synchronizing time with others. For example, the French study pointed out that teleworkers and retired people still made many phone calls in the evening because (apart from the cheaper tariffs) that was when other people whom they called were at home. In general communications between adults and their (sometimes retired) parents also took place in the evening. The qualitative part of this French study showed how calls earlier in the day were often redirected to the evening since people wanted a quiet period to deal with phone conversations at more length (De Gournay and Smoreda, 2001). Social codes in some countries also imply that one should not phone after 10.00 p.m. (Lelong and Beaudouin, 2001).

Another French study showed that even Internet users avoided going online in the early part of the evening. They did this both to keep the (single) phone line free for incoming and outgoing calls and because the early evening was more often devoted to family times, like having a meal together. Internet traffic rose after 10.00 p.m. Prior to that, sessions online were shorter (Lelong and Beaudouin, 2001).[3] That particular research went on to examine experiments using terminals other than the PC for accessing the Internet. As regards using a set-top box to access web-TV, the television watchers in the household would usually impose their timetable on when the TV set was used for viewing broadcast programmes and when it could be used for accessing the Internet. Meanwhile, web-phones were used for the Internet only after 10.00 p.m., when ordinary voice phone calls were no longer made.

The influence of time, and timing, on ICT consumption can be further exemplified from the results of a British qualitative study of managers and professionals attitudes to and use of cable TV.[4] Whatever the actual level of interest the particular household members had in television, work commitments, children and lifestyle choices meant that the majority of the interviewees often had at best only a few hours to watch TV during the weekdays and at weekends. Many of the men, especially, worked long hours at their place of work. After coming home they expected to spend some time with their families. So parents from this social class would often not have the chance to begin viewing until 8.00 p.m. or later – and then some of these would be going to bed by 10.00 p.m. or 11.00 p.m. It is therefore understandable that many argued that cable was not justified because they did not have time to watch much TV, or enough TV.

Staying with this example, it is also worth considering one of the selling points of cable – the number of films it offered. In the time slot noted, these managers and professionals could in theory have fitted in watching a film. However, many of this group also liked to watch the evening news as a priority, either (during this period in the mid-1990s) at 9.00 p.m. or at 10.00 p.m. This in turn meant that the other TV programmes they watched (including ones they videoed) were of shorter duration than a film and they were viewed either side of the news. In other words, the timing of their commitment to the news, and wanting to see it live, blocked the option to watch a film.

One last example of the constraints on the timing of ICT use relates to social expectations about communication. There are the social codes as regards replying to emails and text messages. As already observed, the technological promise is that one can reply when it is convenient, offering temporal flexibility. However, in practice there are often social pressures to reply sooner rather than later, as observed by participants in the European P-903 study. This is captured in comments such as 'I feel obliged to communicate' and 'The sender often expects a fast reply' (Klamer et al., 2000). We saw earlier in Chapter 3 on children and youth how they sometimes felt under pressure to respond quickly to the gift of a communication.

In fact, this pressure can actually lead to a sense of losing control, and even a counter-reaction, as was described by a female participant in a British qualitative study (Haddon, 2000c):

I'd say that 40 per cent of the email I get at work is social, I also get an incredible deluge of work-related stuff. Now my social email is just out of control, over the last two years there's just been more and more of it, it's so tedious ... my email circle has increased and they're getting more frequent ... it's quite outrageous and takes up far too much of my time, it's becoming quite annoying, I used to reply straight away, now I leave it for weeks on end without replying because I just can't be bothered with it any more.

One might ask more about the factors that put pressure on people to reply, the expected timescales of replies and how people respond to these pressures in practice. This example also draws attention to the way in which the practices of textual messaging might change over time as people engaged in this type of communication decide to respond differently.

Blocks of Time versus Fragmented Time

One further question concerns whether people can find blocks of time for using ICTs, and how large those blocks are, versus the degree to which the time for ICT use is fragmented. This issue has been discussed in relation to gender, where women, who still have more responsibility for domestic labour, experience relatively more fragmented television viewing then men. They often fit viewing in between other activities. But the picture is made more complicated by other factors. In a qualitative study of teleworking, both male and female professionals, for whom work was a career and a priority, organized work into blocks. This was because they needed protracted periods of concentration in order to carry out their tasks, and it was reflected in the timing of their use of ICTs such as the computer. Meanwhile, clerical telework was predominantly undertaken by women who were trying to earn some extra money for the household while being at home. Work, and hence the use of ICTs, was temporally more fragmented as these teleworkers alternated between small tasks (e.g. printing off) and domestic chores (Haddon and Silverstone, 1993).

This issue of the duration of time slots allotted to ICT use can be important for a number of reasons. In a French study of experiments involving ADSL (broadband), the researchers argued that its flat-rate tariff was actually one crucial factor leading people to devote longer blocks of time to the Internet. They did not worry about the costs associated with pay-per-use. The authors thought that this contributed to more sophisticated usage,[5] and that spending longer blocks of time online facilitated learning. In fact, in comparison to narrowband access, more people in these households learnt to use the Internet, in addition to the main expert (Lelong and Beaudouin, 2001).[6] We might speculate as to whether having blocks of time for ICT use also allows for more experimentation and a greater chance of achieving success (e.g. in terms of finding what one wants on the Net).

How attentive are people when experiencing fragmented time? The phenomenon of multitasking – doing several things simultaneously – would be a relevant example worthy of further investigation. The fact that many women multitask because of their degree of involvement in domestic labour has been discussed in various studies. But more generally, the increasing saturation of households with ICTs has led to many people consuming several technologies at once. We might think of the examples of listening to music or TV while being online, or children switching between doing homework on a PC and instant messaging with friends. To take one slightly older example from television, we might consider the practice of zapping between programmes using the remote control and keeping track of several narratives simultaneously. To what extent have we trained our attention to cope with such practices?

Perceptions of Time

There has been some research looking at perceptions of time and ICTs. For example, people's 'orientation' to time (past, present and future orientations) can have a bearing upon ICT consumption (Silverstone, 1993). The television schedule can be used to mark, or give a sense of structure to, the passing of time (Scannel, 1988).

But one theme from the time literature has been only occasionally linked to ICTs, and that is perceptions of time stress or the sense of time pressure that people sometimes mention (Klamer et al., 2001).[7] In this section we stand back from technologies for a moment to think more generally about how this time stress has been conceptualized and explained as well as to reflect upon factors shaping perceptions of the quality of time. One can at least ask whether such perceived pressure has a bearing upon the perceptions and roles of ICTs. For example, under what circumstances and for whom can ICTs help to alleviate a perceived time stress problem? Or when are they seen as contributing to that problem, leading to more pressure?

Time Stress

Time stress is a theme in the wider literature on time, also expressed as 'time famine', 'the time squeeze' or the 'harried leisure class' (Southerton, 2001). An apparent paradox commented upon in some of the time literature is that while time budget data have demonstrated that those in employment have gained slightly more leisure time (or rather 'non-work time'), surveys show that people actually feel more time pressure.

There has been a range of explanations for the widespread experience of harriedness (reviewed in Southerton, 2001). Some of these make reference to objective changes in society. While claims that we work longer are empirically not true, other changes in our time structures provide more plausible explanations for this sense of being harried. One of these is the weakening of socio-temporal structures as more work takes place at different times, as we can shop at different times, etc. While this provides more individual flexibility on the one hand, it can also increase (time) problems associated with coordinating with our social networks (this theme is followed up later – Southerton, 2001).

Then there are a range of explanations referring to people's changing time strategies, themselves based on new expectations. For example, one account referred to the amount of things people now tried to achieve. In a German study, three-quarters of those surveyed said that they experienced time pressure precisely because they were trying to do too much in their leisure time (Garhammer, 1998b). Another changing strategy involved the speeding up of life as people did things more quickly in order to fit everything in. Hence, leisure activities become less 'leisurely' (Roberts (1976), discussed in Southerton, 2001). In this respect, ICTs may themselves contribute to this faster pace of life, as observed by this Italian interviewee in the European P-903 study (Klamer et al., 2000) when he observed: 'New technologies allow you to do more activities but they make you frenetic and stressed.'

Apart from the sheer number of activities undertaken it has been argued that the duration and frequency of these activities are changing. This leads to people feeling time pressure because they use their time more intensely, perhaps doing several things at once, or because the large number of separate activities leads to a succession of short, frequently changing episodes of activity (Bittman, 1998). Multitasking has also been cited as a cause of stress. Or if not actually doing several things at once, then at least 'juggling' activities has also been mentioned in this respect.

The Quality of Time

Two arguments about the perception of being harried introduce ways of thinking about the quality of time. The first comes from a UK qualitative study, which argues that although people referred to the idea of time stress when asked to comment on their own everyday life, in practice their days were not stressed overall (Southerton, 2001). But what emerged was the fact that there were particular periods when they felt harried because they had packed many activities into a short time frame, which the researcher called 'hot spots'.

This compression of activities can be caused by the pressure to fit in with the time structures of institutions, as in the rush to get children ready for school in the morning. Hot spots can arise from the problem of coordinating with social networks, occurring when there are small windows of time in which to make contact. They can arise due to the unpredictability of events which mess up plans. But hot spots can also arise because of the desire to fulfil a different time strategy: to create 'cold spots'. The examples of cold spots provided by the study's participants were characterized in terms such as 'quality time', 'potter time', 'chill time' and 'bonding time'. In other words, because people wanted to create times which had a special quality, ones which were not under pressure, they allocated their daily practices unevenly, dashing around (during hot spots) to get the task out of the way in order to create periods of calm.

The second, Australian, study started out with the literature suggesting that women felt more harried than men (Bittman and Wajcman, 2000). However, many of the studies cited to support this claim were qualitative in nature and so the authors wanted to check these arguments using time budget data. Overall, there was not much of a gender difference in terms of aggregate leisure.[8]

But the researchers argued that leisure unaccompanied by a second activity (i.e. with no distractions) was of a different quality from leisure constrained or 'contaminated' by such secondary activities (such as having to monitor children, or modify leisure preferences to fit in with children). Males were far more likely to experience the first, which the researchers called 'pure leisure'. This was shown when the data for primary and secondary activities were combined. Women were more likely to experience their leisure combined with unpaid work.

Second, the researchers looked at the average maximum duration of episodes of pure leisure. This was longer for males. The average number of pure leisure episodes was greater for females, meaning that female's leisure experience was more fragmented into periods of shorter duration. Arguably, this was less relaxing than unbroken leisure.

Finally, the researchers developed the concept of 'adult leisure', defined as time spent in pure leisure or 'intense leisure' (primary and secondary activities both counting as leisure) without the presence of children. If children were present, this time would be designated 'family leisure'. The gender differences were most notable when the children were very young. Mothers' leisure was mostly family leisure, while fathers had at least some more time for adult leisure.

The various approaches used in this study attempted to demonstrate, statistically, that the quality of leisure time was different for males and females. In conjunction with arguments from qualitative studies, this helped to explain the greater female perception of being harried.

Given the lack of available evidence, it has been possible in this section to illustrate only some of the ways in which the issue of time perceptions has been approached and in particular to think about the quality of different times for different people. It remains an, as yet, unanswered question as to how that subjective perception may have a bearing upon how we experience

ICTs. Do these technologies become associated with times perceived as stressful, or with the high quality times described in these two different studies? And how should we assess ICTs in the light of such perceptions (e.g. as time-saving/shifting and hence stress relieving; as helping to create hot or cold spots; as contributing to that stress, as when we make ourselves more reachable by others)?

Planning and Managing Time

Although in the previous section we saw some examples of the way people manage time (e.g. creating hot and cold spots), compared to the amount of data on time use there is actually very limited research on the detailed practices of time planning and on the different temporal strategies open to us (Chatto, 2001). Research of this kind would need to cover practical questions such as how people adjust their schedules, renegotiating plans in the face of contingencies. For example, if something overruns do people dispense with the end of the activity or do they move the whole time plan for the day? It would need to cover how people adapt time plans to each other (e.g. comparing time schedules, by trial and error), how much they are aware of other people's time plans and how much time they spend communicating about these plans.

As reported in Chapter 3 on children and youth, German research from the late 1980s discussed the changing experience of childhood during the twentieth century (Büchner, 1990).[9] It traced the decline of street culture, where interaction was to some extent spontaneous with peers who happened to live nearby. We saw that more free time was spent not only in the home but also at a distance from the home both in after-school institutions and also with friends who lived at a distance. This German study made the point that maintaining such social circles required more coordination and planning, and children became more dependent on being transported by adults. In this context, the telephone became more and more essential not only to arrange meetings, which could be partly done at school, but also to confirm them after negotiations with adults. Children, it was argued, were experiencing a more intense time economy, often having to say they had 'no time' and finding themselves under more pressure to 'save time'. This process became part of their socialization into later adult roles. The children learnt to manage their time economy, schedule activities, arrange appointments and make commitments to others. It also implied that the timing of meetings required more advanced planning and was less spontaneous (e.g. compared to simply going to the house of somebody who lives locally).

Subsequently, research on the mobile phone has suggested that this technology can produce the opposite effect, creating more spontaneity. French research described the shift in appointment-making practices as people could now call someone if they happened to be nearby in order to see if they could meet up (Licoppe and Heurtin, 2001). Meanwhile, Norwegian research discussed the way people used the mobile phone to make arrangements to meet after they have already arrived at a destination such as a pub, restaurant or other site. They improvised a meeting rather than planning one in advance. The research observed this behaviour was especially developed among teenagers, as well as the practice of only vaguely specifying where to meet at first but then progressively firming this up through subsequent calls (Ling and Yttri, 2002). A slightly different take on a similar process came from a Japanese study noting similar mobile phone communication in the build-up to a meeting and then further communications by mobile between young people immediately after the meeting (Ito and Daisuke, 2003). This made the meeting even more 'fluid'.

Thus, in contrast to the fixed-line phone research described earlier, such uses of the mobile phone (as well as phoning ahead to warn that one is late and rescheduling when underway) imply the need for less planning in advance. They suggest more spontaneity or flexibility in organizing meetings and travelling to them. Indeed, the teens in the Norwegian study explicitly acknowledged this ability to organize meetings at the last moment. So has this led to new 'just-in-time' forms of socializing (to borrow a term from the field of production)?

To answer this, it is worth considering a point made earlier about the problems of synchronizing time with others, including other family members (especially as people's individual time schedules become more varied). This was captured in one of the European P-903 focus groups by this Danish male participant: 'When we were younger, we visited each other spontaneously. We don't do that any more. Now we call in beforehand and make appointments'. Another French male participant complained about the constraints of family life: 'With a child ... we need to plan everything. We cannot go out any more. With the new means of communication, we may organize things better but we feel like we are in a restraint'.

The point is that the greater possibility for instant communication does not necessarily lead us to change the way we plan and manage time. It is more difficult to do so at short notice, more spontaneously, if we are locked into some of the time structures that have been discussed at several points in this chapter. Clearly the Norwegian youth referred to earlier would seem to have had a fair amount of flexibility in this respect – but not everyone does.

Conclusions

The issue of disposable time is important because to the extent that we reserve time for other activities, this in turn limits or shapes the consumption of ICTs. Sometimes the anticipated time costs of ICT use are enough to shape decisions and people even give up use because of time costs. While examples of this have emerged anecdotally and in qualitative research, such considerations appear not to have been examined more systematically – providing scope for investigating whether time costs are an issue for some groups more than others.

On closer inspection, we need to look not just at the amounts of disposable time available to use ICTs, but also at issues concerning the timing of that use and the time structures of people's lives. Despite the promise of some ICTs to allow us flexibility by time-shifting, this is only partially realized because of the constraints of our time structures. Hence, one general research question concerns the degree to which the time structures discussed previously are flexible or inflexible. In other words, under what circumstances, for whom, and in relation to what type of (social) constraint are people freer to change the time order of their daily lives? If we consider the theme of blocks of time for ICT use or whether that use is fitted into more fragmented time structures, we might go on to ask about people's freedom to determine the duration of time slots devoted to ICTs. To what extent does being able to organize blocks of time have any beneficial effects?

Subjective perceptions of time have received some attention in the sub-literature on time, especially in the debates about the causes of time stress. Two lines of analyses were picked out in this chapter because they provided a way to think about the 'quality' of time. Arguably research into this subjective dimension is worth pursuing since people's evaluation of their time, and their evaluation of how ICTs are affecting it, may well influence their adoption and use of these technologies.

There appears to be an even more limited amount of research on the actual way we plan time use more generally, about the mechanics of planning and about time strategies. More information about this would be needed in order to appreciate whether various ICTs fit in with, assist or are at odds with the way people actually go about organizing their time. While we can pose the general question asking how much ICTs have had an impact on such planning processes, we can ask a more specific one about whether they are providing more or less scope for spontaneity of action.

Notes

1. This was a middle-class sample since at the time of the study in 1998 the predominant users of the Internet had this profile.
2. The French analysts examined communications traffic from France Telecoms' data, the survey material and in-depth interviews from a variety of projects from a programme of research on communication and life cycles (see Chapter 8).
3. This article represented a synthesis of the results from four years of French experiments on access to the Internet.
4. This study consisted of in-depth interviews with twenty households, half with and half without cable TV. It was conducted in 1995–6 for the cable company Telewest (Silverstone and Haddon, 1996a). The households were from social class AB.
5. Other factors influencing experimentation included the rapid response through using high-speed access.
6. More women and more elderly people used ADSL compared to narrow-band.
7. There are national variations in perceptions, reflecting perhaps not just different objective circumstances, but also different expectations. For example, in surveys asking working people if they felt rushed, 25 per cent said yes in Germany compared to 11 per cent in Spain (Garhammer, 1998b). Second, even within countries, there is variation. Certainly those involved in what has been called more 'passive' leisure activities (e.g. TV watching) have not necessarily felt pressured nor, surveys suggest, have young workers spending time in pubs, cinemas etc., whose social life involved a large amount of social communication (Garhammer, 1998b). Third, being busy does not necessarily mean feeling stressed. Even sections of the population who experience a crowded timetable might agree that they are, or outsiders might define them as being, busy – but they need not experience this as pressure. For example, some find that being busy is stimulating. In the European P-903 focus group study, those participants who had both mobile phones and Internet access were more inclined to talk about the huge number of different activities which made them live an active and rather hectic life, including in their leisure time. But these people often liked to be busy, they did not feel stressed but saw being busy in a very positive way (Klamer et al., 2000). Others also have commented on the fact that being busy can be symbolic of a 'full' and 'valued' life (Darier (1998), cited in Southerton, 2001).
8. The researchers used multinational data for the overall figures and Australian data for the more detailed analysis of combined activities.
9. This chapter was based on a literature review, combined with data from a youth survey.

7

Movement, Public Spaces and ICTs

Our relationship to space, like time, has a bearing on how we use and experience ICTs. While the issues around locating ICTs in domestic space and the implications of this will be covered in Chapter 9, this chapter examines two other spatial relationships. The first, admittedly less rooted in the traditional interests of the domestication framework, concerns ICTs and movement through space, i.e. how ICTs relate to various forms of travel behaviour. The second deals with how ICTs are experienced in public spaces.[1]

Starting with travel, it has been pointed out elsewhere that mobility has been a relatively under-researched topic within the social sciences, or seen only as a black box where the nature of and social motivations for travel have received little attention (Urry, 2000).[2] In certain respects, this is also true of travel and ICTs. Therefore, in comparison to the other chapters, this chapter cites less evidence but poses more research questions.

The chapter starts by drawing upon historical studies that suggest ways in which wider social changes may have set the preconditions for the reception of ICTs. Could changing travel patterns be one such social change? In particular, how might changes in the travel patterns of particular groups such as children and women have a bearing upon their ICT acquisition and use? Why is it important to disaggregate travel behaviour into different types of mobility?

We can also ask about the opposite causal relations. How do ICTs affect patterns of travel? For example, do new ICTs that facilitate teleworking or enable e-commerce have implications for mobility? If, as discussed in Chapter 6, new patterns of interpersonal communication made possible by mobile phones have changed our patterns of meeting, what implications has this for patterns of movement? How do ICTs themselves influence the very organization and management of travel? Specifically, how are newer ICTs such as the mobile phone and email making a difference in this respect? What of the new travel information services becoming available – what research questions would we want to ask of their take-up and influence on travel experiences?

Apart from influencing the motivations for and logistics of travel, ICTs can have a bearing upon the very experience of mobility. For instance, in what ways do ICTs enable us to manage our affairs remotely, when away from home? How do they affect how we make use of travel time? How do they alter what it means to be abroad, as well as what it means to be away from home? How do they influence how we feel about travelling?

To set the scene for the second main topic area of this chapter, 'public' and 'private' are constructed notions referring to different things in different contexts. One common approach has been to refer to the public world of work and the private world of the home. However, some analysts have wondered whether the two notions are themselves changing, partly aided by new ICTs like the mobile phone. For example, what counts as public and private communications may depend less on the particular place and more on the form and purpose of communication (Cooper et al., 2001).

This section of the chapter focuses mainly on expectations of and behaviour related to mobile phone use in different social spaces outside the home. It takes up the traditional interests of domestication research concerning how people manage their relationships with others through and around ICTs. But it looks outside the home to ask what strategies people have developed for managing their mobile phones in public spaces and how they interact with the other people who are present.

The Effects of Mobility on ICT Use

Changes in mobility can set the preconditions for the reception of new technologies.[3] Raymond Williams once argued this in relation to the spread of certain ICTs in the UK at the start of the twentieth century. He maintained that the spread of photography, gramophones and cinema as well as the growth in popularity of media such as newspapers reflected the greater geographical (or residential) mobility that was occurring at that time as people moved to live and work in different locations (Williams, 1974). This led them to take more of an interest in these 'new' ICTs (as they were then) that preserved memories and helped those who had moved to keep in touch with what was happening in their birthplaces. In other words, he argued, changing social experiences made the time period especially favourable for these new innovations. The same type of argument could be suggested here.[4] In this case, we might speculate (as did Townsend, 2001) that growing mobility in everyday life has helped to create the positive reception given to a range of ICTs, including mobile phones and certain aspects of the Internet. It has done so through giving rise to more occasions when such ICTs could be perceived as being very useful.

If we move beyond general mobility in society, we can ask how current patterns of mobility among different social groups might affect ICT use. For example, in Chapter 3 we saw that children's patterns of mobility are complex and involved parents ferrying their children to various venues. So one question is whether the issues of logistics that this necessitates has contributed to parents acquiring mobile phones for their children (as well as for themselves).[5]

To take another example, we have the relation between mobility and gender. To a degree, previous constraints on women's travel have been reduced as women's greater entry into the labour market has increased pressure for second cars or for shared use of cars (Salomon et al., 1993). Since statistics have consistently shown that women were more likely to say that they acquired the mobile phone for emergencies – including the car breaking down – there is the question of whether this mobility trend contributed to the take-up of the mobile by women.[6] There are other issues arising from the particular nature of women's mobility and its implications for ICTs. For example, research has also observed that women often combine more trips through a number of different spaces when travelling compared to men (Turner and Grieco, 2000). Do the logistics involved have any bearing on the adoption, use and usefulness of mobile phones?

Another way of focusing research is to disaggregate different forms of mobility. The frequency and duration of different types of travel vary, as does their regularity in terms of occurring more or less routinely or spontaneously. Both in its planning and execution, travel takes place with different degrees of difficulty. Trips may be motivated by a variety of social obligations and commitments. The extent to which they occur through an individual's (perceived) 'free choice' also varies. Travel entails different levels of pleasure and stress. In other words, rather than talking just about movement or mobility in general, it is also important to disaggregate the various forms of travel if we are to appreciate their importance and meaning and hence, potentially, the different roles that ICTs may have in relation to these travel experiences. Two examples – commuting and travel abroad – are provided to illustrate such differences and to show what research questions could be asked about how they may influence ICT use.

In one sense commuting is not such a large part of the total amount we travel – it constitutes about 20–25 per cent of total mobility (Jansen, 1993). But it is strategic in a number of senses. It is the main form of mobility around which other travel is fitted, thus determining the timing of these other trips. Commuting has increased due to the greater participation of women in the labour force. Meanwhile, the distances commuted have grown across Europe since the early 1980s, reflecting the process by which populations and jobs have become increasingly decentralized (Jansen, 1993).

There appears to be a limited amount of research, at least in the public domain, about the effects of commuting on ICT use. But we can at least pose some questions to explore how this particular form of travel may have a bearing upon interest in these technologies. Partly anticipating a theme to be discussed later, in what ways and for whom have commuting problems meant that transport information systems or traffic news (delivered by various means) have become tools for aiding commuting decisions? Where there is uncertainty about how long commuting will take and if such travel is strategic in terms of fitting in with other journeys, what bearing has this had upon the use of mobile communication – voice telephony or otherwise – as a tool for coordinating with others? To ask a question pertinent for telecommuting, for whom and to what extent do problems specifically related to commuting influence decisions to use ICTs in order to spend at least some time working from home?

Turning to the case of international travel, the number of trips abroad made in 1989 was five times more than in the mid-1960s. International travel has filtered down through all the different socio-economic levels of the population (Potier et al., 1993). Travelling abroad may not be, literally, 'everyday' mobility for most people. But the P-903 study showed that it was much appreciated, apart from becoming easier (Klamer et al., 2000).

From various qualitative studies we see examples where people who are abroad use not only fixed telephony but also fax machines and email (including from Internet cafés)[7] as well as mobile phones to keep in touch with their children and parents back home. But one could imagine research exploring more systematically the communications practices of people when they are abroad. This could include asking more generally how people use portable ICTs when they are abroad – ICTs ranging from more work-related laptops to more leisure-orientated devices such as music-playing equipment, portable interactive games and audio-visual devices. For example, to what extent do people take such ICTs with them and use them when they are abroad in order to bring some of their familiar world with them?

ICTs Affecting Patterns of Travel

This topic has taken on an added salience in the light of ever greater concerns about the environmental unsustainability of current levels of mobility, or what has been termed 'hypermobility' (Adams, 2000). The question asked from this perspective is whether the use of ICTs in various respects could reduce the need to travel. The complication is that 'green' concerns are not the only consideration. Indeed, some have asked whether high degrees of mobility form part of our fundamental experience of modernity (Sørensen, 1999).

Turning to specific ways in which to reduce mobility, the topic of telework started to gain publicity in academic circles in the early 1970s when the energy crisis led US researchers to consider 'telecommuting' as an alternative to physically commuting (Nilles, et al., 1976). The environmental agenda has continued to foster the particular interest in whether ICTs used for work purposes could reduce some need for travel (e.g. Gillespie et al., 1995; Anderson, 2001), even if there could be other motivations for teleworking or for allowing teleworking.[8]

One factor to bear in mind is that telework is difficult to measure because of different researchers' definitions of the phenomenon, its invisibility and, for many, its unofficial and casual nature. If we count those who work mainly from home, the number is relatively small (Gareis, 2002), not the huge percentage of the workforce predicted by some enthusiasts. On the other hand, if we consider more occasional telework, such as one day a week or less, the numbers go up. While the implication for travel is obviously less than full-time teleworking, there may still be some effect.

Perhaps the tricky question concerns the role of ICTs in causing any such telework to happen. Policy documents and research papers mention the potential role of technology drivers, most recently the Internet (e.g. Gareis, 2002). However, there is the question of how influential the technological developments are compared to other factors. Research from the early 1990s before the widespread adoption of the Internet suggested that at best the influence of ICTs on the decision to telework was mixed (Haddon and Silverstone, 1994). Some people worked at home anyway, and the arrival of newer ICTs simply made their life easier. At the other extreme, but more rarely, new ICTs enabled telework that could not have taken place before. In fact, the findings of much of the research into people's and firms' motivations for taking an interest in teleworking indicate a lesser role for technology. While it may offer the potential to work at home, it is the managerial, economic and social considerations that are usually more important in shaping actual decisions. These include the willingness of companies and other employers to allow teleworking and the choice made by workers to take up this option.

The development of home-based online transactions such as home shopping and telebanking offers another potential way to reduce the need for travel. However, the five-country qualitative study of the Internet showed that even when people used services such as online shopping facilities, some of them also combined this with physical shopping (Haddon, 1998c). For example, they sometimes checked prices online and then bought the item from a shop. Or they went to a shop to see a product before buying it at a cheaper price online. This in part reflected a preference that many people have for physically seeing an item before purchase. This is also the reason why some people resisted remote purchasing altogether. Some shoppers, in relation to some goods, take pleasure in physically shopping, and people still liked to get out of the house at times.

On the other hand, that same qualitative research suggested that for some people, especially at busy times, the option of remote purchasing could be attractive and useful. In addition, routine shopping, purchases of some immaterial services and purchases where the physical nature of the good was less important (e.g. compact discs) could be handled remotely with less concern. One common worry in this 1998 study was the perceived lack of security on the Internet as regards credit card transactions. Many interviewees had encountered media stories of Internet fraud, and so, even if they knew that fraud using only the basic telephone was possible, they thought that there were more problems with the Internet. However, if we take the payment element out, a number were willing to look for products online. Meanwhile, telebanking was enjoying some success.

So the picture is mixed. These new services are useful for some purposes, but they do not automatically replace all existing consumption practices. Moreover, much of the research on e-commerce has not been directly inter-ested in the implications for mobility. One concern that is sometimes raised about practices such as home shopping is that any large-scale growth of these remote interactions might mean that people will become more home-centred and lose a certain amount of social contact (Klamer et al., 2000). In other words, the fear is that we may become too immobile.

Finally, there is the question of the effect of ICTs on travel for the purpose of making social contact. We saw in Chapter 5 on social networks that contact via the Internet can lead to particular cases of travel to meet people that might otherwise not have taken place. It is unlikely that this is really going to make much difference to people's overall mobility. As regards the mobile phone, in Chapter 6 on time we saw instances when people were out of the home and they used the mobile phone to ask someone else to join them, perhaps leading to a journey which otherwise might not have taken place. But as in the case of Internet-based transactions, one might speculate that this has a relatively minor impact on mobility in general.

In sum, any evidence we have about whether ICTs themselves lead to less travel or more travel is often only glimpsed, arising anecdotally, in studies with other agendas. Or else it is seen in exploratory studies.[9] But even lacking the quantitative and systematic evidence to explore some of the mechanisms outlined here, it is clear that there are grounds for doubts about the extent to which new ICTs, or rather the practices related to them, have had a substantial effect on travel.

ICTs, the Organization of Travel and Management of Daily Life

In Chapter 3 on children and youth we noted the German study that showed the increasing use of the fixed-line phone by children for arranging meetings with peers (Büchner, 1990). A more recent French ethnography documents the equivalent usage among young adult friends (Manceron, 1997). Qualitative studies indicate this process continuing with the newer ICTs (Haddon, 1999a; Haddon, 2000c; Klamer et al., 2000). We find, for example, email being used in the longer term planning of meetings such as family reunions or parties, its advantage in comparison to voice telephony being its ability to broadcast details and even maps to several people at once.

While Internet-based email can be used for planning more short-notice events such as meeting up after work, delays in the arrival of messages and lost emails have been acknowledged as being a problem (Haddon, 2000c). In this respect, the mobile phone has an advantage.[10] For example, talking about mobile voice telephony this British interviewee observed: 'It's really useful to check up where people are on Saturday nights and they know they can get hold of me' (cited in Haddon, 2000c). Making similar comments about text messaging and youth, this 17-year-old Norwegian interviewee commented: 'On Friday there are a lot more text messages than on Thursday because people are out and need to find out what is going on' (cited in Ling and Yttri, 2002). Qualitative studies have also shown instances of using the mobile phone to confirm meetings (in order to avoid wasting time if there has been a change of plan). They have been used to help overcome problems of locating people one is supposed to meet up with in public spaces (i.e. phoning to ask where they are), and, frequently cited, they have been used to warn of delays and the need to reschedule.

Mobile telephony and texting not only help people to organize meetings but also facilitate people's ability to manage the logistics of everyday life. In their concept of 'micro-coordination', the authors of a Norwegian study included calls to arrange for children to be picked up and dropped off as well as calls contacting people when they are underway in order to arrange for them to take on some other activity, such as going to the shops (Ling and Yttri, 2002; Ling, 2004).

Apart from such interpersonal communication, the information provided by ICTs can itself have a bearing upon patterns of mobility. For example, we might consider the role of the Internet in the initial stages of planning a journey (e.g. checking routes, travel options), organizing the relevant transactions (i.e. buying tickets) and checking relevant travel information at the last minute to see if there are problems (e.g. road traffic congestion, rail delays, flight delays). For some time it has been possible to plan journeys and check for problems using teletext (at least in some countries such as the UK) as well as monitor certain travel conditions by radio (e.g. traffic congestion problems). The Internet has since provided yet another means for managing our travel, as have the car radios which actively search for traffic information, the mobile phone services for cars supplying information on traffic conditions nearby, the computer software for route planning and the public transport touch-screen information services.

One can also imagine research questions about who chooses to use the facilities in the list above, in what circumstances and for what forms of travel. Equally, why and by whom are they not used? But maybe it is more appropriate to think of people having a repertoire of information sources just as they have a repertoire of communications options. People already draw upon various sources of information in planning travel, including word-of-mouth advice, anecdotes told by others and personal experiences. Hence, the better questions to ask might be: when do people take on new sources and how do they fit them into the set of existing travel information resources open to them? Turning to the consequences of ICTs, do such information services make the planning of travel more or less time-consuming, involve more or less effort, more or less stress, or lead to the development of more skills in planning? And do they save time actually spent travelling (on occasions when those time-savings are desired)?

Finally, mobile phones have influenced not only the organization of logistics but also our ability to manage our private affairs when away from home. One of the earliest US studies of the mobile phone introduced the concept of 'remote mothering'. This referred to women carrying mobile phones in order to be available to children when needed, to be able to continue 'mothering work' even when they were not physically present (Rakow and Navaro, 1993). The theme of mobiles making us more available has been raised by participants in subsequent studies, as when they observed that their mobility was no longer constrained by having to stay at the home base to wait for messages (Mante-Maijer et al., 2001; Palen et al., 2001)

ICTs' Influence upon the Experience of Travel

We now explore the experiential dimension through a number of different worked examples.[11] The first is travel in terms of spending time abroad. Credit cards increasingly allow people abroad to draw money from ATMs (cash machines) without having to deal with banks or bureaux de change when they need to change money. The growth of mobile phones means that there is no need to use, and learn how to use, the telephone systems of the country one is visiting. Developments such as automated kiosks that provide tourist information with multi-language options allow us to discover things in our own language. The availability of local information on the Internet provides those (going) abroad with a new way to find out about their surroundings. These examples illustrate the point that one is using a familiar interface, there is less need to know the language of the country, less need to know the particularities of how things work there, less need to work out how to find things out – i.e. to discover the social system. It may be more convenient, but without being nostalgic we can simply observe that such developments change the very experience of being abroad

Being abroad, whether on holiday, for business purposes or as part of a longer visit (e.g. for study purposes), not only means coping in a different environment, but also means taking a break from the daily interactions, commitments and routines associated with being at one's main home. However, ICTs make it increasingly easier to maintain those links, to be in contact, to know what is going on back home and to be reachable. Consider how satellite provides access to more foreign TV, which means some travellers can watch their own national TV when abroad. Meanwhile, mobile phones and the Internet cafés allow us to stay in touch. In some respects such developments have enabled those who travel or spend a longer time abroad to perhaps have some peace of mind and continue to manage their lives and relationships with others when they are away. The other side of the coin is that such options potentially change the experience of having a break.[12]

The second example involves the use of travel time. Qualitative research has indicated that some people find it quite useful to be able to utilize mobile phones to exploit travel time, to fit in those calls that it is more difficult to make at other times. If travel time is perceived as 'dead time', or a boring time, then people welcome the chance to be able to do more with it, either using voice telephony or sending text messages (Klamer et al., 2000). Presumably the same is true of other portable ICTs.

However, it would be misleading to think that all travel time, even commuting, is experienced in this way. For example, one study by the French Ministry of Transport showed that for some people the time spent commuting was their only free time to reflect, and they were concerned to keep this time.[13] In the later P-903 study, some participants used travel time for reading books or newspapers, or planning daily activities (Klamer et al., 2000). Commuting could also be useful for allowing a mental transition between home and work or for simply relaxing. In other words, the subjective experience of travel time and how we want to use it is diverse. The implication is that we should consider more carefully what activities and experiences the use of ICTs potentially displaces.

The third example involves feelings of security when travelling. One of the clearest instances of this, cited in various research, is the greater sense of safety provided by mobile phones. This is often mentioned in relation to driving, and is perhaps more acute for some groups than others – e.g. the Swedish Handicapped Research Centre found that disabled people felt safer with mobile phones when driving alone. In an early survey women certainly indicated that they felt safer when driving because of the mobile (Rakow and Navaro, 1993).[14]

But driving is not the only example. Having the mobile phone available can provide a general sense of security and assurance, a degree of peace of mind knowing one has more options to respond, as well as reassuring others, such as parents (Ling, 2004). The same point could be made not only for actual travelling, but also for being especially in isolated places, such as the Norwegian second home in the country (hytte), often located in remote places 'near to nature' (Ling et al., 1997). Not only having the phone but also talking while passing though public spaces and even making sure one is seen using a mobile in public can provide a sense of security. Whether it does lead to more actual security might be open to debate (Ling, 2004).

Finally, we have a very different type of subjective experience of mobility in terms of comforts and pleasures. Entertainment-related ICTs in particular would be relevant here, if one considers the rise of in-car entertainment, for example. One British study of the Walkman explored the various ways in which personal stereo use can be used to 're-spatialize experience' (Bull, 2000). Using familiar sounds to accompany them on urban journeys meant that people had a sense of never having left home and they could ignore the environment through which they passed.

ICTs in Public Spaces

Understandings about the degree to which physical (and always social) spaces are deemed to be relatively more public or private are subject to ongoing negotiation.[15] So too are expectations about appropriate behaviour in such spaces. There may well be some institutional definitions of the status of certain spaces and of (in)appropriate behaviour in them and even regulation of those spaces (e.g. no smoking, no begging, no playing music instruments, no using a mobile phone during performances). Yet people still have to work to make those definitions stick, to make that governance of space a reality. Moreover, those definitions and that regulation are sometimes resisted. Or else new situations emerge, such as the arrival of new ICTs, which pose afresh questions of appropriate behaviour and of the nature of different types of space.

To take an example of this last possibility, we can consider the arrival of one of the first portable entertainment ICTs – the Walkman. Early reactions to its use in public space by those co-present were particularly negative, as were those of some social commentators. Analysts trying to make sense of this reaction drew on the anthropological perspectives of Mary Douglas. They argued that this private listening in public spaces was 'out of place' and thus transgressed boundaries (du Gay et al., 1997). The authors of this study added that with the proliferation of this particular technology, the negative reaction to the Walkman diminished somewhat over time. But similar reactions, partly for similar reasons, were later directed at the mobile phone.

Arguably, the disruptive nature of new ICTs in public spaces has been even better exemplified by the mobile. For example, in the mid-1990s when mobile telephony was first developing as a mass market, the European Telsoc quantitative research showed that sizeable minorities still had quite negative reactions to mobile use.[16] Even by 2001, qualitative and quantitative European research in the P-903 project was still showing perhaps a surprising degree of negative reaction, though perhaps understandably more so among those without mobiles (Mante-Meijer et al., 2001).

While there have been some attempts to explain this reaction in terms of the nature of mobile calls (e.g. the disruption of the ringing, hearing one side of a conversation) several studies have referred to people's expectations of communicative behaviour in public spaces. For example, one argument has been that any code of conduct that had emerged in relation to the fixed telephone was now disappearing through the 'chaotic and divergent' use of the mobile phone (de Gournay, 2002).

In addition to such arguments about public space in general, we need also to think about the particularities of different spaces. Certainly the European Telsoc quantitative study found varying degrees of willingness to turn on mobile phones in different types of space (Haddon, 1998a).[17] In fact, in order to understand the reactions of those co-present and the behaviour of users, various studies have attempted to specify the more detailed meanings of particular social spaces, going beyond the blanket concepts of public and private. For instance, we saw how one Norwegian study looked at the hytte, or holiday home, as a space for taking a break from city life and for communing with nature (Ling et al., 1997). Admittedly, the mobile phone sometimes played a role in enabling that break, by allowing people to be contactable in emergencies or for work. Yet it also presented a problem to be managed by users. It threatened to disrupt the essential desire to make a break with normal daily life. To cope with this, mobile users negotiated with potential callers and family the conditions under which the mobile could and should be switched on or off. However, such negotiations were not always easy. Other analysts have also observed that one can be called to account by others for not switching the mobile on (Cooper et al., 2001).

Meanwhile another Norwegian study, this time of the restaurants,[18] explored the very particular expectations people had about what was involved in going out for a meal, constructing private spaces within a public setting that should not be disturbed (Ling, 1997, 2004). The research documented the negative reactions and subsequent actions of those co-present when a mobile call was taken in this setting. As in the case of many authors researching this topic, this analysis drew upon the vocabulary developed in Goffman's work for describing ways in which everyday life is like a theatrical performance.

Such studies remind us that although the focus has been on 'space', we really need to be attentive to time-space, to the 'situation', to the 'moment' and to the social activity that is taking place.[19] For example, it is not just the fact of being in restaurants that may have a bearing on how we feel about and handle communication. Rather, it is the act of going out for a meal with someone, reserving a time as well as a space for them, with all the expectations and desires that this may imply.

Strategies for Managing Communication

The importance of the desire for privacy when making calls was emphasized in the European Telsoc quantitative study when it looked at the prevalence of different strategies for securing privacy when using the basic telephone (Haddon, 1998a).[20] This search for privacy re-emerged in two studies of public telephone kiosk use. The first, a French study, observed that some people used kiosks because they had no access to a fixed line at home. Other users did have such access but instead preferred to use public phones because they wanted privacy from other household members (e.g. younger people did this in order to escape parental surveillance) (Carmagnat, 1995). A similar finding emerged in a second, Japanese, study of younger people who used public phones because of the lack of privacy at home (especially because it was very easy to hear phone conversations through the thin walls in Japanese homes) (cited in de Gournay, 1996).[21] Both studies provided examples of a public space providing (for the caller) more privacy than the home. This can also be true of mobile phone use (Ling and Helmersen, 2000). In the European Telsoc study, 14 per cent of the whole sample said that they had used the mobile phone specifically because it provided some privacy (Haddon, 1998a).[22] However, in researching the use of the work phone for private purposes, one French study found that only certain types of communication were felt to be appropriate in the work context – i.e. there were some subjects that would not be discussed in such phone calls (de Gournay, 1997). It remains to be seen how the nature and content of calls influence people's willingness to make such private calls in different types of public space.

Just as Chapter 4 provided examples of people's strategies for controlling contact via the fixed line, so too there are strategies for controlling incoming mobile communication. For example, apart from switching off their phones in different social locations, qualitative studies have indicated how people turn the phone off when it rings or let it ring. Both actions can direct calls to voice mail (Licoppe and Heurtin, 2001, 2002). We should add that in addition to wanting to control their overall reachability, people sometimes want to avoid giving out the contextual details of where they are, what they are doing and the presence of particular others.

The caller is not the only one the mobile user needs to manage. Various studies have revealed the strategies that mobile users adopt for dealing with co-present others, be they known or strangers. These include trying to be discreet when answering calls and moving to a separate space (Bassett et al., 1997). If they want to demonstrate to others that they care that they might be infringing expectations, mobile users may indicate that they are trying to deal with this by 'speeding up' the call to bring it to an end more quickly (Licoppe and Heurtin, 2002).

Yet other analyses of the messages we give to bystanders draw upon Simmel's (1997) characterization of the anonymous urban experience and how we try to cope with what has been described as the 'inflicted co-presence' of other people. Portable ICTs such as the Walkman (Bull, 2000), the laptop or palmtop, handheld games and now the mobile can all be used to cut us off from those immediately around us. Using a mobile, accompanied by signals that include avoiding the gaze of others and the use of gestures and body movements, can tell other people about the user's non-availability and serve to create a private bubble within public space (Cooper, 2000; Cooper et al., 2001).

Conclusions

Changing patterns of travel may have set the general preconditions for the reception of ICTs. In addition, the examples of children and women's mobility suggest that there is some scope for exploring whether the mobility of different socio-demographic groups have consequences for ICT adoption and use. However, it is important to disaggregate the different types of mobility since the potential role of ICTs might vary in relation to these different types of travel.

When we turn the question around to ask about effects of ICTs on mobility, the issue can be approached at a number of levels. Many of these parallel the questions asked about time in Chapter 6. One first consideration is how ICTs influence the activities we take on, the way we link activities and hence the patterns of movement between activities. For example, do the options provided by ICTs such as mobile telephony enable us, indeed tempt us, to pack more activities into the day? Clearly such a question relates to the wider issue of time use, the timing of activities and the 'busyness' of life. But it also has implications for mobility. A second level also refers back to a theme of Chapter 6. How have ICTs affected the planning of mobility? For example, how much in practice do people seek out travel-related information, how much has this changed and why, when and how does it make a difference to travel decision-making – with what implications? Here the issues of spontaneity of time planning discussed in Chapter 6 once again have implications for mobility. A third level of analysis concerns how ICTs can have a bearing upon the subjective experience of travel, as exemplified by changing the experience of being abroad or being away from home, the experience and of using travel time for other purposes and the sense of security or pleasure ICTs bring to the travel experience.

The main research issue as regards the use of portable ICTs in public spaces is their potential to infringe expectations and understandings about appropriate behaviour in different social (times and) spaces. While the earliest studies were of the Walkman, most recent attention has been on the mobile phone. It is possible to imagine this issue extending to the use of ICTs such as camera phones and mobile videophones. In each case, there is scope for further research to pin down the specific issues relating to each technology, the expectations relating to different public spaces, strategies for managing the technology and any related communication and interactions with co-present others. This task has already begun.

Notes

1. This chapter is largely based on a review undertaken within the European action COST269. The report of the COST269 Mobility Workgroup, 2001, is to be found via http://www.cost269.org.

2. In fact, Urry (2000) calls for a 'mobility turn' in the social sciences, making different forms of mobility (not only corporeal mobility) more central to sociology's core interests. Indeed, more research into this field has started in several European centres.

3. When discussing how the arrival of the telephone influenced wider social change in the USA up until 1940, Fischer describes the difficulty of disentangling the effects of the take-up of a particular technology from that of other technologies and from other non-technological factors (Fischer, 1992, p. 264). This note of caution needs to be borne in mind here, and applies equally to the task of distinguishing the effects of changing travel patterns from other influences.

4. This type of argument about changing social contexts favouring take-up of the mobile phone has been made in relation to changes other than in mobility. For example, it has been argued that changes in the public sphere and forms of sociability aided that success of the mobile phone (de Gournay, 2002).

5. Certainly parents participating in a Norwegian qualitative study observed that the mobile had helped in this respect (Ling and Yttri, 2002)

6. For example, the European Telsoc five-country study, in 1996 and a 1999 survey for British Telecom's Digital Life Programme.

7. See Lee (1999).

8. For example, that it allowed flexibility for employers or for the tele-workers. (For a fuller discussion of motivations related issues about the experience of telework see Haddon and Lewis, 1994; Haddon and Silverstone, 1993, 1994; Haddon, 1999b).

9. An exploratory quantitative study in Norway followed up this qualitative analysis, exploring how much and in what ways mobile phones affected (certain types of) mobility (Ling and Haddon, 2003). The results suggested that on balance mobile phones did not generate more trips (although the fixed line did). However, the study also discussed the problems of interpreting these data and what steps might be required for more sophisticated research.

10. A similar advantage is shared by the telephone. For example one Swedish study showed that email use by elderly people was far more

likely to be restricted to long-distance messages, with the phone being used for such things as coordination of meetings (Östlund, 1999).

11. Here we should consider a range of portable ICTs, including laptops, palmtops and organizers. Although we are starting to find research on the details of how these ICTs are used for business purposes (O'Hara et al., 2000), there is less on their social use.

12. Perhaps this is most dramatically demonstrated in the case of students living abroad where email especially has meant that they are kept constantly informed about what is going on back home, lessening the extent to which they are truly away from home.

13. Personal communication from Chantal de Gournay.

14. In a slightly different sense, Bull discusses how personal stereo users can have a sense of being more 'secure' in terms of feeling at home and at ease in public spaces because of the sense of familiarity which the music brings (Bull, 2000).

15. Although the interest in this paper is in relatively public spaces, the ongoing work of creating relatively public and private spaces within the home for the purpose of making different types of telephone call on the fixed line is described in Lohan (1997). For a discussion of some varied meanings of terms such as private, see Livingstone (2002, pp. 161–2).

16. In the 1996 survey there was some variation between countries, but, for example, in Italy, in the UK and in Germany over half of the respondents said they had some negative thoughts when mobiles were used, either in terms of being annoyed or thinking that the user was showing off. The percentage was slightly smaller in France and in Spain where mobiles were less widespread at the time (Haddon, 1998a).

17. For example, to take the two extremes, there was a greater willingness to have them switched on in the (relative privacy of the) car. Mobile phones were most likely to be switched off at a play or show. The other spaces about which questions were asked in this survey were the home, restaurants/bars, shops, buses/trains and other people's homes.

18. What type of restaurant, and hence what type of social space is involved, makes a difference. The same point is made in a Japanese study: while young people would be willing to take voice calls in a fast-food restaurant or family restaurant they would be less willing to do so in a 'fancy' restaurant (Ito and Daisuke, 2003). Of course, there may also be culturally specific factors at work, with a French study noting that all those interviewed turned off their phones in restaurants in general – maybe reflecting something about French culture (Licoppe and Heurtin, 2001). Meanwhile, Italian research involving observation

on trains made a related point. Different kinds of trains constituted different social contexts. For example, high-speed long-distance and local trains were different from each other by virtue of the people who used them and the duration of the journey. They certainly generated varied patterns of mobile usage (Fortunati, 2003).

19.   To add yet more complexity, Italian research has drawn attention to the need to consider not only types of social space but also whether one is in company, whether the space is familiar, whether one is known in that space, whether one is making and receiving calls, etc. These can all influence mobile phone behaviour (Fortunati, 2003).

20.   The strategies researched were moving to another room to make a call, calling when nobody else was at home and calling from somewhere else outside the home. To give some idea of how important this was, in most countries about 40 per cent said that they phoned from another room. In keeping with Chapter 3 on youth, younger people used this strategy more often.

21.   As we saw in Chapter 3 on children, this was underlined in a later Japanese study pointing out the relative smallness of Japanese homes, and the fact that young people rarely had private rooms, but often shared a room with a parent or sibling. Having a second phone line was also rare, largely because of the expense. This, it is argued, later contributed to the particular popularity of the mobile phone (Ito and Daisuke, 2003).

22.   This was the weighted figure for Europe, allowing for differences in population between countries. There were small variations between countries (e.g. in the UK this figure rose to 19 per cent) and younger people were more likely to mention this (in the overall sample over a quarter of 14–24 year olds referred to the privacy role of the mobile phone at a time when the mobile phone was not so widespread (Haddon, 1998a).

8

Changing Life
Circumstances and ICTs

Our longer term relationship to ICTs can alter, be that in terms of deciding to adopt or give up a technology or to use it more, less or in different ways. This chapter deals first with changes in individuals' and households' circumstances. Some of these changes are gradual, some more dramatic, some more predicable and anticipated, some more unexpected. They include somewhat common phases associated with the life course,[1] new work and leisure options and interests, different financial situations, etc. Although such longer term change was not emphasized in those earliest formulations of the domestication framework, it was examined in subsequent research as well as in some other, especially French, studies.

We start with studies looking at changes in the nature of work and household composition. These can have a bearing upon our routines and the organization of everyday life, providing new orientations and creating new demands. Sometimes these transitions are accompanied by changes in financial constraints, perhaps best exemplified by the cases of unemployed people and single parents. How do ICTs become less or more salient as our situations change? When do they take on new roles because of these transformations? When do some of these transitions actually reveal a dependency on ICTs? Or, to refer back to the concerns of an earlier chapter, when do some transitions lead to possible forms of social exclusion through loss of access to ICTs?

Alternatively, and perhaps best illustrated by the teleworking example, how can changed circumstances lead us to adopt new ICTs? In what ways can even upgrading ICTs, such as getting a new computer, have ramifications within the home? How can such changes alter rules and understandings about how we should use existing ICTs?

Shifting focus, as illustrated by transitions related to gender, the birth of the first child and retirement, how do communications patterns via ICTs evolve following the move to a new phase of life? For example, who now makes calls within the household, who is called, who answers calls, and how are the purpose and even length of calls different? We may already have evidence about such matters in relation to the phone. But in principle equivalent questions could be asked about the mobile phone, the Internet and any future media.

The last section deals with experiences that derive not so much from the life course as from the eras through which people live. It explores the changing circumstances of different generations, of different cohorts of people born at different times. How do people's earlier experiences in life, both of technology but also their tastes and orientations, affect their later consumption of ICTs?

Work Change and ICTs

In principle there are a number of ways in which people's work circumstances change over time. Examples would be the number of hours worked, the amount of commuting or whether they have to spend time away from home. All of these can have repercussions for communication practices and for the use of ICTs. Here we look at two examples. The first comes from a late1980s German study of unemployed people and the phone, referred to in Chapter 2 and now examined in more detail (Häußermann and Petrowsky, 1989). The second is from research conducted in Britain in the early 1990s on teleworkers' use of ICTs (Haddon and Silverstone, 1993).

The Transition to Unemployment

The German researchers pointed out that, under conditions of longer term mass employment, unemployed people had more chance of getting back to work through utilizing informal networks and actively seeking work rather than by going to job centres. Therefore, as people became unemployed it was important to stay in touch with various social networks by phone. Through this medium they could find out about work opportunities, could be recommended by personal acquaintances should a vacancy occur, could make informal enquiries and could be contactable by potential employers. Even if they were quasi self-employed, the phone could be important for managing to get some employment in the informal economy. It was useful for such administrative demands as sorting out pensions and other benefits or finding out what documentation to bring to social security interviews.

Apart from its role in relation to seeking work and sources of income, the phone could be a significant resource for finding out about special offers when trying to manage on reduced finances. It could be a means through which others could provide psychological support, especially given the stigma that can accompany the loss of work and because unemployment can be a very individualized experience. Ultimately the phone was just as important for unemployed people as for anyone else in terms of making arrangements to meet with others. They may have had time to spare, but they still needed to synchronize it with others and hence plan their schedules. It was often through the phone that people were invited to a range of social events such as coffee gatherings, sports or family celebrations, etc. Without a phone it was easy to drop out of society.

This study, although involving a limited amount of quantitative data, has a wider salience. The researchers made the general point that while the phone had enabled geographical relocation and new forms of social networking, it had at the same time become a necessary condition for maintaining these networks and patterns of contact. The more widespread the phone had become, the more difficult it was to be without one. The researchers used this argument, that the phone was nowadays important for citizenship, to make a case for the state provision of phones and perhaps some state support for the costs of usage. Clearly this relates back to Chapter 2 on unevenness of ICT access and how lack of a commonplace ICT can lead to forms of social exclusion.

However, some of the arguments could equally well apply to groups not necessarily thought of as 'the unemployed'. One example would be the women who choose to leave the labour market because of the arrival of children and who, perhaps as 'housewives', have less public visibility, certainly in official employment statistics. Many of these points would also apply to those who become low income earners, even if they are still working. These observations often apply to those who become single parents (to be discussed later). Many of these take up some form of state benefit because of their children, and hence they are not technically classified as unemployed. They too could all too easily drop out of social networks. This is why they appreciated the phone because it enabled psychological support under difficult conditions.

The Transition to Teleworking

The British study showed how the move to working at home was sometimes a catalyst for acquiring new equipment and services such as faxes, answering machines or email. Sometimes these were 'free' in that they were funded or loaned by an employer or client. The British study indicated how some teleworkers, who would never have thought of acquiring various ICTs for purely domestic purposes, could now justify these purchases because of their work. Only subsequently did they discover other personal and domestic uses for the technology.[2]

Teleworkers faced the problem of controlling the boundaries between home and work. One specific facet of this problem was that of impression management. The teleworkers from the early 1990s study were often conscious of the need to present themselves as competent and professional. This meant conveying the image that they were operating in conditions convivial to work in order to convince employers and clients that home life was not a distraction. The phone became much more of a device for managing such impressions. It was used to portray the home as a workplace. Sometimes this led teleworkers to install separate phone lines, not only to avoid blocking the work phone line with social calls, but also so that teleworkers knew how to answer work calls, how to present themselves. Or else the addition of answerphones allowed teleworkers to time-shift telephone calls to moments when they could prepare their presentation and avoid background noise – especially that made by children.

Where a second work phone line could not be economically justified, as in the case of some clerical self-employed teleworkers, the existing domestic phone took on an additional role as a work tool. Hence, rules concerning its use often had to be renegotiated. It was important to avoid blocking the phone line at certain times with social calls when this might prevent work calls arriving. Or else telework led to new regulations about phone use. These covered who could answer it and when, what they should say, how they should develop a telephone manner and how much noise could be made in the vicinity of the handset.

The consequences of impression management extended beyond the phone. Once the home became a place of paid employment, existing ICTs were located, in effect, in a new context, a new environment. Managing the sound regime of the home sometimes became an issue. TVs and audio equipment not only threatened to disturb the teleworker's concentration when working but also allowed domestic life to make its presence felt. The distractions of home ceased to be contained and hidden away when the teleworker answered phone calls or dealt with visitors. As a result, these existing media sometimes had to have new constraints imposed upon their use. They had to be played more quietly or only at certain times. Lastly, teleworkers were sometimes conscious of the need to demonstrate symbolically to outsiders and even to other household members that they really were working, and not just unemployed or housewives by virtue of being at home. Reorganizing and calling the space where ICTs were located a 'home office' was one strategy employed to achieve this effect. In which case, ICTs were now orchestrated as objects of display. It was not just what they did but how they looked which became important.

Where equipment was supplied by an employer or client there were sometimes very clear rules as to how the work tools such as PCs should be used and by whom. But especially when teleworkers bought their own ICTs for working at home, this gave both partners and children new access to these technologies and services. Although allowing children access to the PCs used for work could create worries about the damage they might cause, many teleworkers nevertheless encouraged children to use work PCs for word-processing or the development of keyboard literacy. If the study was repeated nowadays we might expect to see these teleworkers promoting 'Internet literacy' and the use of the Web to support school homework. In other words, in a process characterized in that research as 'technological seepage', the introduction into the home of new technologies for work could affect the technological culture of the household as whole, providing opportunities for other members of the household to gain new skills.

But that study also found forms of what it called deprivatization, whereby the introduction of work ICTs had implications for social relations outside the home. On the one hand, ownership of photocopiers, computers or faxes became seen, albeit in some cases only in a limited way, as a sharable resource. Acquaintances would ask to use the technological resources in the same way as neighbours might ask to borrow a cup of sugar. A later study of Internet use indicated that friends, family and others sometimes 'borrowed' access to the Internet in the same way (Haddon, 1998c). In addition, several teleworkers in the study reported how they had been asked to actually produce something for outsiders on their computers and other equipment. In this facilitative deprivatization the teleworker provided technological services to the wider community (or extended family).

Changing Household Composition and ICTs

Developments over the life course (or life cycle) lead to changes in household composition. Some are more commonplace, as when new members arrive (e.g. are born) or depart (e.g. as children leave home, or through deaths). These transitions can have multiple implications for ICT use. For example, when children leave home they are simply no longer present to use the old home phone, but now that phone is used to stay in touch with them.

Certain changes are experienced by only a minority of the population. One example would be the move to more communal living, with various degrees of social closeness involving non-kin (e.g. sharing a flat) and kin relationships (e.g. three-generation households). Such changes also shape the particular ways in which ICTs and communications of various sorts are managed (see Lohan, 1997, on households of friends). For example, in the British studies on the early to mid-1990s, various interviewees discussed the effects of having new, non-family members join existing family households – such as au pairs and lodgers – which often forced them to rethink the rules about phone use and paying bills.

As in the case of the work transformations, a particular example from 1990s British research will be used to explore what can be one of the more dramatic examples of changing household composition: the move to single parenthood, especially with the break-up of families (Haddon and Silverstone, 1995a). That study dealt mainly with the fixed-line telephone (and media such as the TV). But arguably it could have relevance for newer ICTs.

The Transition to Single Parenthood and ICTs

Following the move to single parenthood, the basic phone became much more of a lifeline to the outside world. Without another parent available to go for assistance, the phone became more essential for emergencies or for critical moments, such as when the children were ill. Even in the mid-1990s some slightly more affluent single parents were considering buying mobile phones in order to be even more reachable or to deal with contingencies (e.g. if they were delayed in traffic when coming to pick up their children).

There were also some basic practicalities. The single parents in the British study commented on the flexibility that the basic phone gave them in terms of negotiating childcare with friends and with ex-partners. They could more easily change arrangements by phone at shorter notice rather than having to plan far in advance their childcare plans or their ex-partner's access to the children. For those who managed to lead a more active lifestyle in their social networks, the phone was simply important for coordinating activities with others.

In the study it was clear that the basic phone had also become a social lifeline. This was partly because of the need felt by many single parents to talk though the aftermath of family dissolution. But it was also because of the isolation that single parents often experienced as they were trapped in the home in the evenings through having to stay in with the children. If such a study were to be repeated now it would be interesting to see if the Internet could offer any benefit in this respect. As a mode of communication it is in many respects more formal than the intimacy offered by voice telephony. However, one can think of the various self-help and mutual support groups that nowadays form online to put people in contact with others in a shared position or predicament in order to discuss experiences and solutions.

However, whatever the potential of new technologies, that same study also pointed to barriers to their use. Either due to the household no longer having two incomes, or due to the dependence on state benefits, many single parents (coming from family break-ups or not) possessed limited financial resources.[3] This restricted their ability to afford new technologies. In some cases basic ICTs, like other goods, were hand-me-downs, gifts or second-hand. Or else other people, especially extended family members, provided access to such technologies.

Many of these single parents experienced a certain amount of stress from economic and social reasons. Their priority, especially immediately after family break-up, was to sort out their (new) lives. In the early 1990s, computers and other technologies did not come to mind as being relevant for many single parents, as their horizons were limited by current social circumstances. That said, as life settled down, such ICTs could come onto their agendas. But for a time this particular transition could create barriers to adoption and use.

Life Course Changes and ICTs

French research has stressed the important influence of changes in the life course upon communication patterns. To explore these, the late 1990s saw a series of studies being conducted covering youth leaving home, families moving house, single-parent families and retirement.[4]

One general review of the French empirical data on fixed phone use drew attention to the fact that as young single people formed couples and started families, they had increasing contact with parents and decreasing contact with friends (Smoreda and Licoppe, 1999). For instance, as couples formed there were more calls between the individuals in the couple to manage everyday life. At the same time, the number of calls to the friends of the two people before they formed a couple decreased by half. Meanwhile calls to family members doubled, and increased yet again once children arrived. Only when people grew older and lived alone again did they once more start to increase the amount of telephone contact outside the family.

In keeping with the approach taken in the rest of the chapter, the next section considers three examples in more detail. The first comes from a French analysis of the five-country Telsoc survey data looking at how gendered use of the phone developed over the life course (Claisse, 2000). The second is from a French project (part of the programme already noted) looking at the effects of the birth of the first child on patterns of sociability via the phone (Manceron et al., 2001). The third is from a British project from the mid-1990s looking at the consequences of the transition to retirement (Haddon and Silverstone, 1996).

Changing Gender Telephone Behaviour over the Life Course

The first French study, analysing the data from the 1996 European survey, looked at a variety of changes in phone use over the life course (Claisse, 2000). The first two factors considered were (a) the main user of the phone in a household and (b) the main 'call answerer'.[5] Initially, young males and females had a fairly equal inclination to phone. This continued to a large extent as they formed couples without children. The pattern changed with the arrival of the first child. The domestic telephone was used more by the mothers than the fathers. Moreover, once the children had grown up and left, the pattern of women being the main users and call answerers persisted (among those aged 60–69).

The next step in this study involved a factor analysis of three variables – the duration of calls, the aim of calls and the person spoken to – in order to build up a picture of the evolution of gender practices.[6] The phones calls of people aged under 25, and who were still living with parents, were oriented to social networks of friends. Compared to the parents, this age group used the phone less for getting information, more for chatting and organizing activities. As they grew older (from 14–17 to 18–25) the pattern was broadly the same, but the older group had more activities to organize. The only gender difference at this stage of life was that girls had slightly more communication with their family, and had slightly more interest in chatting, while the boys emphasized organizing activities a little more. Girls' calls lasted longer because of this.

The next stage was when people left home, either as single persons or to form couples. As before, single persons mostly called friends, but family calls rose somewhat as these young people passed on news to their parents now that they had left home. Having nobody to talk to in the new home, these single people used the phone more for chatting, for passing time with others. Their calls were longer than when they used to live with parents. Although this was a shared gender pattern overall (i.e. the male and female patterns were relatively close compared to some other life stages), the female singles tended to have more chats and longer calls.

Thinking of the group aged under 35, as they formed couples but before children arrived there were fewer calls for chatting, reflecting the fact that the couple could now talk to each other in the home. The calls therefore became shorter. There were relatively more calls to organize daily life. The couple also now had two families to keep in touch with. At this stage the male changed his behaviour more. His calls to work colleagues increased and he now used the phone mainly for organizing his activities. His calls were now shorter than before. Females continued to use the phone just as they had done when they had been single, for chatting, exchanging news and passing time.

With the arrival of a child, practices evolved once more. In keeping with the theme developed in more detail in the next example, family became more important than friends (which remained the pattern for the rest of their lives). As the children grew older there were some further changes. Work life and non-work interests ('associative life') gained in importance. The female, as we saw, often became the main user and the main call answerer (in households where there was one person fulfilling that role). The arrival of more children did not change the male's behaviour compared to the previous stage. Females, whether economically active or inactive, spent less time chatting on the phone and more time organizing daily life compared to earlier. Their communications became shorter, and they managed calls to the rest of the extended family.

Once the children had left home and the couple reached 60 there was a final change. With the end of working life, their children setting up home and the arrival of grandchildren, calls become more social, less about managing daily life. Since time constraints had become less strong, they were flexible and more time was available for chatting and sharing news on the phone. The phone also became a means of passing time rather than managing it. For those reaching widowhood, calls became even longer. For the male, for the first time since being single, calls were mainly for chatting and passing on news. For the first time in his life, calls to family became the most important ones. With no more working life, he recentred on the family, although calls remained brief. Claisse (2000) called this period the 'feminization' of the phone, and hypothesized that it reflected the way in which masculine identity had been thrown into confusion by the end of paid work.

The Birth of the First Child and Changes in Communications Patterns

The French researchers in this second study stressed the fact that the dependence of the child upon its parents had a profound effect on their interactions with their friends and family.[7] This entailed a reorientation of 'telephonic sociability' (Manceron et al., 2001).[8] The researchers argued, based also on other research, that the social support network was at its lowest level at this point in the family cycle. The new family became self-sufficient and centred in upon itself, reorganizing life around the child and taking on new temporal rhythms.

During pregnancy in the twelve weeks before birth there was a strong increase in telephone calls (up 25 per cent). After birth this gradually diminished reaching its former level after twelve weeks. But then traffic continued to decrease. However, these aggregate data concealed changes in the pattern of communication. There was no decline in family calls. The parents of the couple remained the main contacts, but a range of family ties were also altered, as grandparents become great-grandparents and the brothers and sisters of the couple become aunts and uncles.

In general, having a young baby led to a reduction of calls overall and a reduction in the number of people called. However, intra-familial calls to the new parent's partner (at work or by mobile) increased. These were often of a functional nature and to coordinate activities. Meanwhile, the young parents simply had less disposable time for friends as their priorities altered – some interviewees explicitly drew attention to this. At this point, the friends were often sorted and put into some form of hierarchy. Acquaintances were seen less often and friends were frequently divided into those who appreciated the changed circumstances of the new parents (e.g. who let the new parents choose the time to make contact) and those who did not. This was often a division between those friends with children themselves or who anticipated having children, and those without children or who were single. Such changes were not irreversible. They were often seen as transitory because the parents anticipated that as the children grew older, they would impose less constraints on the parents compared to newborns.

The parents now had more contact with those in a similar situation to themselves. There were more calls to friends with children than to friends without. One also sees examples of greater contact with previously more distant family members who had children, as well as contact with more distant acquaintances (especially wives of the husbands' friends who have children) because they had similar experiences and shared the same rhythms of life.

Time slots were established so that friends knew when it was best to call the parents, or when it was best for the new parents to make a call. The parents used filtering strategies more, such as letting the answering machine initially take the call or seeing the number of the caller, in order to prevent intrusions (especially when they were doing something with the child, like giving him/her a bath).

This study also started to consider the role on the newer means of communication. The mobile phone was increasingly used to announce the birth immediately after the event. Email was used to spread the news to wider social circles. In terms of the time slots for communications discussed above, email also provided the new parents with more room for manoeuvre, given that the parents had more flexibility in terms of when to send or receive messages. In fact, email was thought to be perfect in the post-natal period when the women were based at home. Email was also useful for sending baby photos to show the baby's development.

Many of those interviewed acquired mobile phones either during pregnancy or in the period shortly after birth to help reach their partner in case of emergencies, to organize tasks relating to the infant or to contact the babysitter or crèche. In other words, at this point in their life they modified their perceptions of how to use the different modes of communication.

The Transition to Retirement and ICTs

There are a few preliminary observations to make about this particular transition. It is by no means a homogenous experience: there are different retirement 'careers' or 'trajectories' (Haddon and Silverstone, 1996). The transition can be more or less gradual (with a sudden end to paid employment at retirement age limits, or a steady decline in hours worked over time). It can be more or less expected (e.g. with sudden early retirement as a form of redundancy), and people respond to it in different ways (e.g. spending more time on activities in couples, having more contact with family members such as children and grandchildren, or finding functional alternatives to work such as voluntary work and roles in various associations). They also face different constraints, both in terms of health and fitness, but especially in terms of the financial gap between those who have occupational (or other personal) pensions and those living just on state pensions.

Turning now to the implications of retirement for communications, a number of the participants in this British qualitative study found they used the home phone more. This was caused partly by the fact that they no longer had access to a work phone, whereas they used to make some social calls from the office – more often for organizational purposes rather than chatting. Now they had to make such calls from home. In addition, many of the participants said that they made more calls nowadays than before retirement because of the new roles they had taken on, for example, involving greater contact with their own families. Despite the general pattern of withdrawal from organizing social activities discussed earlier, some people phoned more because they led an active retirement in terms of taking on roles on committees, etc.

But the pattern of phoning after retirement was not a static one. There were family changes that coincided with or followed retirement. Sometimes these increased the number of phone calls. For example, some of the young elderly made more supportive and social calls to their own parents and relatives, who were perhaps now living alone or who had become increasingly frail.

On the other hand, the death of those elderly relatives could then remove the need for such calls.

Another transition was in the cases where children left home – that too could lead to new patterns of phoning. Some adult children continued to live nearby, which generated local phoning, often to organize meetings. Others moved further afield reflecting generally greater geographical mobility compared to a generation earlier. This led to the spatial dispersal of extended families, including dispersal abroad – generating longer distance and occasionally international calls. Finally, there were health changes during retirement. Even when friends or relatives lived relatively near, the onset of physical mobility problems could mean increasing reliance on the phone.

This study, conducted in 1995, took place at a time when the mobile phone and Internet were only just starting to develop as mass markets. None of the participants had either technology. Nor, at the time, did they show a great deal of interest in them. The one exception was for those who travelled by car. Concern about breaking down had led them to consider, or acknowledge at least, the emergency use of the mobile phone. A later section discusses a particular barrier to Internet use – their resistance to computers.

So how had things moved on after a few years? The P-903 European survey in 2001 found that more and more older users (over 60 years old) had adopted the mobile phone in the later diffusion groups. The majority of the elderly people who had done so had actually taken out a subscription themselves (as opposed to receiving the mobile as a gift). By that time, nearly a third of the 65–74-year-old age group across the European countries had acquired the technology. Moreover, the fact that the curves showing a general decline in mobile adoption by age had become less steep and the levels were so high in a country like Norway (where the whole population had a high level of penetration) suggested that in principle the young elderly were not resistant to getting mobiles. Indeed, given the increasingly active lifestyle of these young elderly people, especially compared to previous generations of young elderly, one can imagine how mobile phones could have benefits for them (Mante-Meijer et al., 2001). In stark contrast, among this same 65–74-years-old age group on average across the European countries only about 8 per cent of the respondents were Internet users at this time, with about double that level in Denmark and the Netherlands.

The Changing Experience of Generations

It is common to hear observations that each younger generation has a different experience through growing up with new technologies. But it may be equally useful to look beyond childhood in order to consider how different cohorts of people are born, grow up and live their adult lives at certain historical periods, encountering technologies and services at different points in their life course. In other words, we have to ask not only about the technologies that people encounter in their youth, but also about the ones they meet when they reach early adulthood, when they form partnerships and perhaps families, when they reach middle age, when they retire and when they enter the latter end of their lives. The demands and circumstances of each of these life stages can have a bearing on what these technologies can mean to them. In this context, one can imagine how relatively easy using mobile phones can appear as an extension of the familiar phone. Although in 1995 many people could not see whether the device was really useful or worthwhile enough, they could at least manage to use one. The design of the handset terminal was less of a problem.

In addition, the social context in which different cohorts had grown up and passed through during their life course help to shape their habits and routines, their values and tastes – and hence their very perception of what different technologies can offer. To consider both of these dimensions, the encounter with technology earlier in life and the shaping of habits or values by previous experiences, we return again to the example of the British young elderly study.

Technical Experience of Generations: The Young Elderly

In the case of this generation of young elderly, many first became familiar with the basic phone through work as this technology became an increasingly common tool in many jobs, especially in the expanding white-collar sector after the war. The majority of the interviewees were both familiar and at ease with the phone. They often compared this with the unease of their own parents for whom the technology had arrived later in life. In contrast to the phone, this cohort of people was not on the whole a computer-oriented generation. Many of those now nearer to being 75 years old had not lived through office automation during their working lives. Others had actively tried to avoid computers at work. Being very near retirement age they had not been enthusiastic about taking on new ways of working and learning computer skills at this stage in their lives. While there were some elderly computer adopters in that study who had been used to the technology at work, for most the computer was beyond their horizons. This was not only because it would be technically difficult to master but also because these elderly people could not envisage how they would fit the technology into their lives and routines.

Two points have to be made about the P-903 survey findings a few years later. Apart from the fact that it is a European and not just a British study, in the six intervening years more of the survey's 65–74–year-old age group would have experienced both PCs and indeed the Internet or email in a work context. Given that the findings show that 8 per cent had adopted the Internet by 2001, that suggests considerably more interest than was being expressed in the mid-1990s. Maybe that is not surprising given the high visibility of the Internet in those intervening years. On the other hand, if that figure is still low compared to the mobile phone, part of the reason might be the fact that among this cohort there remained many for whom computer-based ICTs still represented a huge technological leap.

Values, Habits and Tastes of Generations: The Young Elderly

Many of this generation were from working-class backgrounds. They had undergone upward social mobility in their own lifetime as middle-class occupations expanded. Therefore, it was common to have lived as a child in somewhat austere conditions from the pre-war era into the early post-war years. Although they had enjoyed more affluence from the 1950s onwards, in certain respects they retained non-consumerist values. Participants in the British research would often talk about 'knowing the value of money'. They were careful spenders, interested in getting a 'good deal'. They often resisted rushing to buy the latest version of a commodity, and they had always been more inclined to replace items only when they were sufficiently worn out. Coping with a fixed and somewhat reduced income was not necessarily too much of a hardship for this cohort: they had managed before and they knew that they just had to be careful.

All this led to a certain degree of conservatism as regards acquiring newer ICTs, including telecoms ones or additional facilities. On the whole, people of this generation were not impulse buyers, and acquisitions had to be justified. They had to have a perceived usefulness. In interviews, this age group argued in terms of not 'needing' any more equipment, facilities or services rather than not 'wanting' them. They would often point out that they had been without all the various new facilities now on offer so far – and they had managed. While some were more adventurous, most clearly did not want to try too much experimenting at this stage.

That said, if the usefulness of a technology or service could be demonstrated to them, and it was relatively straightforward, then it could be considered. For example, many had acquired VCRs late in their life, often after retirement. In fact, French research on recently retired people tends to support this. The researchers argued that this group were very likely to adopt new technologies (the mobile phone or the Internet) provided that the 'utility' of these technologies was felt to be compatible with the individual's way of life (Eve and Smoreda, 2001, cited in Mante-Meijer et al., 2001).

Lastly, many of the interests of the young elderly developed in their earlier years. For instance, participation in the Second World War or taking holidays abroad affected tastes for and appreciation of media programmes concerning history and travel. Although the Internet was not widespread when this study took place, a later Japanese study of elderly people online observed hat some of the messages they posted referred to experiences from their earlier life. These would have been understandable to peers who had lived through the same era (Kanayama, 2003).

Conclusions

We have seen how changing circumstances can alter the importance of ICTs, as illustrated especially by the transitions to unemployment and single parenthood. The latter indicated how some technologies could move, albeit temporarily, beyond the horizon while others become more important. Indeed, dramatic changes in life such as these can highlight how dependent people have become on certain basic ICTs like telephony.

Clearly, changing circumstances can influence what ICTs we adopt (or give up, if we think about the Internet dropouts discussed in Chapter 2 on unevenness). The teleworking example indicated how ICTs could enter the home because of new work patterns. But it also showed how such work changes can alter the role of existing technologies, such as the phone and computer, affecting how they are managed and who can have access to them under what circumstances. A change in the situation of some household members can ultimately even lead to new competences being gained by others in the home and new uses of ICTs in relation to wider social networks. More specifically, we saw how changes in the life course can lead to different patterns of communication through ICTs, as indicated in the studies of the birth of the first child and of the move to retirement. Despite some years of observations about different male and female patterns of communication, even these turn out to be dynamic, sometimes more and sometimes less distinct from one another.

Of course, there are many other, major and minor, transitions in life that might well make some difference to our experience with ICTs. These need to be at least borne in mind in those studies exploring changing use over time. For example, if we just take the case of work, we might consider the effects of an increase in the travel component of working, including any new requirements to spend time away from the home base overnight. People also gain and lose access to ICTs through changes in the nature of work or as a consequence of the 'overspill work' that takes place when people who are generally workplace-based do some (extra) work in the home.

The other dynamic considered here was the changing experience of different generations. The study of the cohort of people who were young elderly in the mid-1990s showed how their earlier experiences, both technical and in terms of values and tastes, could shape their current consumption, or indeed rejection, of ICTs. Of course, we could in principle appreciate these shared experiences in any cohort of people. For example, if we reflect upon the studies of young people and mobile phones reported earlier, this was the first youth generation to acquire and experiment with this novel technology. Does this mean it will have particular meanings for them in later life? What happens to the use of the mobile by this current cohort as its members grow older and some of the reasons for using the mobile that derived from this particular teenage life stage no longer apply? As their circumstances change, what elements of their practices do they keep and what do they alter (e.g. thinking about text messaging, for example)? Furthermore, how will future generations of youth (or younger children) experience the mobile phone differently once this technology has become more established? In other words, what difference does it make to people's relationship with a technology when they grow up with it (just as generations grew up taking the presence of television for granted) as opposed to being the generation who first experienced it?

Notes

1. We should add that nowadays there is increasing diversity of household forms (e.g. single parent, childless couples, gay or lesbian couples) compared to a 'classical' nuclear family.
2. The same situation occurred in later studies of Internet access (Haddon, 1999a) and mobile phone use (Bassett et al., 1997). Technologies that were sometimes originally acquired for work, or justified by work, were subsequently used more for private purposes. The fieldwork for the study of teleworkers was conducted in 1992 and involved twenty households filling out week-long diaries and then taking part in in-depth interviews. This was reported in Haddon and Silverstone (1993). See http://members. aol.com/leshaddon/Date.html.
3. A later US study of single parents found similar results (Russo, 2003). For example, in surveys single parents were the lowest adopters of PCs.

In the qualitative study some had given up their PCs, or could not find time to use them, and some of those who did have computers had older models.

4. The France Telecom Research Programme, 1998–2001, was called *Cycle de vie, événments de rupture et pratiques de communication* (Life cycle, major life events and communication practices). It consisted of the projects *Décohabitation juvenile* (Youth leaving home); *Déménagement de familles et usage de téléphone* (Families moving house and use of the telephone); *Familles monoparentals et communication* (Single-parent families and communication); *La Naissance du premier enfant et sociabilité téléphonique* (The birth of the first child and sociability on the phone); *Transformation de réseaux et des pratiques de communication à la retraite* (The transformation of networks and communication practices with retirement).

5. In French, *standardiste* means 'switchboard operator'. The question was 'Does the same person usually answer the phone when it rings?' In 90 per cent of households there was one main user, and in 66 per cent of cases this person was female; there was a main call answerer in 45 per cent of households, and in these households 73 per cent were female. This latter finding has a precedent, with another French analyst pointing out that women also open the door more often when the doorbell rings (Mercier, 2001).

6. British Telecom's research noted how the timing of calls is another variable that can change over the life course, e.g. with the arrival of children (Lacohée and Anderson, 2001).

7. There were quantitative and qualitative components to the study. The qualitative one involved interviews 'immediately' after the birth of the child (between birth and 3 months) and then interviews with sixteen people when the child was between 9 and 12 months and with another sixteen people when the child was between 12 and 18 months. Observational studies took place between the age of 6 and 12 months.

8. The same result was found at a multi-country level in the P-903 European study (Smoreda and Thomas, 2001).

9

The Careers of ICTs

This second chapter on the dynamics of our relationships with ICTs begins by considering the social processes associated with the initial arrival of new technologies and services. Obviously the factors affecting the initial decision to adopt technologies are very relevant for understanding the uneven experience of ICTs discussed in Chapter 2 and indeed for appreciating take up more generally. The first section takes a step back from the moment of first consumption to consider the social shaping of technologies. What are some of the wider social influences that help to shape the initial understanding and expectations of ICTs? This is followed by questions concerning the early experience of these technologies. What sources of support facilitate the use of ICTs? If we take the example of the Internet, what are the various processes involved in learning how to use the Net and learning what is useful or fun? How do patterns of use change during the early learning period?

Both domestication research and other studies have argued that particular ICTs should be seen as entering into the ensemble of other technologies, and indeed other artefacts, which already have a place in our lives. So how do the new ICTs fit in with, or rather how are they fitted in with, what already exists? For those ICTs used in the home, how do they find a physical, although simultaneously symbolic, place in this domestic setting? When new ICTs are acquired they are brought into a context where we have developed existing practices relating to the technologies and services we already possess. In which case, how do those pre-established practices have a bearing upon the use of new ICTs? Conversely, how do those new ICTs affect our relationship to the existing ICTs that we use? Such questions provide one route to start thinking about the social consequences on new technologies.

The last section looks at some examples of how our relationship to ICTs can evolve in the longer term. This can help us to evaluate claims about the degree to which particular ICTs are integrated into our lives compared to the extent to which certain uses are contingent. How is our own usage affected by the emerging patterns of use within the wider communities in which we live? How can the arrival of competing and complementary ICTs change our use? How do developments in the technology itself affect our relationship to ICTs? What are the consequences when our existing ICTs multiply?

Learning about ICTs

ICTs can have associated with them varying degrees of symbolic meaning that go far beyond their functionality, especially when they are seen as 'the cutting edge' or 'the future'. One historical example was the wonder that existed, or rather that was created, around early radio. At one stage radio was seen as the marvel of science, delivering sound out of the ether, and there were various utopian predictions about where this would all lead (Douglas, 1986). To take later examples, the initial home computer boom in the early 1980s was boosted by contemporary discourses about the impending information revolution (Haddon, 1988a) and the Internet was associated with the vision of the Information Superhighway.[1] It is important to add that although such symbolic representations of technology may be created and circulated by public figures, futurologists and the media they can also find a broader resonance in the public. This can help to fuel popular enthusiasm, as measured by the amount, the ways and the contexts in which people talk about ICTs in the course of their daily lives.

These social discourses and popular enthusiasms can help to shape expectations, sometimes providing a basis for interest in ICTs such that people acquire them 'for the future of their children' or 'out of curiosity' to 'see what all the fuss is about'. It can lead to what might seem to be a novel (but may be increasingly common) form of consumption: acquiring the technology or service and then working out what to do with it later. This was certainly the case with the early home computer in the UK (Haddon and Skinner, 1991; Skinner, 1994) and appears to have sometimes been the case with the Internet (Haddon, 1999a).

The various agencies, often companies, developing technologies themselves play a role in creating some of these public representations. Or, indeed, they help to change them over time. If we look at the history of telecommunications, at different points in time various national telcos started to actively promote the social uses of the phone, whereas previously it had been regarded within the industry as a tool for serious purposes – in large part reflecting the original limited capacity of the network. In the case of the mobile phone, by the mid-1990s advertising campaigns started to change the identity of the mobile phone from being that of a business tool to being that of a mass market commodity of use to everyone. By the end of the twentieth century the mobile was even portrayed as a fashion accessory.

Research on the home computer in Australia highlighted some manu-
facturers' attempts in the 1990s to change the image of home computers.
They did this by changing the design of the machines to make them look
and feel more like consumer electronics such as VCRs, in terms of colour
and styling (Lally, 2002). The study also outlined efforts to feminize some
products in this way, including iBook, WAP-enabled phones and personal
digital assistants (PDAs) – for example, by making PDAs look like a purse
powder compact or clutch purse.[2] Meanwhile, advertising images portraying
the PC as a kind of domestic appliance that was well integrated into the home
appeared in catalogues alongside VCRs, televisions and even microwave
ovens, as well as in mainstream family magazines and lifestyle magazines
such as *Better Homes and Gardens*.

The media also play a role in framing perceptions of new ICTs. Starting
again with historical illustrations, Australian research covering the early
1900s described how the first radio magazines succeeded in giving radio a
broader appeal, beyond being a hobbyist interest, and helped to establish
the experience and practices of broadcasting (Johnson, 1982–3). In the USA
in the 1950s, TV magazines were important in addressing and helping to
overcome worries about early television (e.g. its effects on children) (Spigel,
1992).

In the late 1970s in the UK, electronics magazines once again played a
role in actually creating a hobbyist interest in early computers by convincing
electronics enthusiasts that microcomputing should be their next major
challenge (Haddon, 1988a). At a later stage, magazines aimed at a wider
audience contributed to the interest that created a mass market. At one
point it was claimed that computer magazine sales were greater than sales
of combined women's magazines. At the same time, contemporary TV
programmes explaining what computers could do helped to foster curiosity
about the technology.

During the 1990s in the UK, but the same is probably happening elsewhere,
we saw something similar in relation to the Internet. For example, a range
of TV programmes explained what one could do on the Net.[3] In the case
of mobile telephony, 2001 saw the launch of a British magazine specifically
for child and teenage mobile phone users (*Mobile M8*) explaining what
was 'cool', what was fashionable, what was the latest, how the language of
texting worked and what fun could be had with mobiles.[4]

Yet such media coverage can have diverse, sometimes negative effects. For
example, one US study argued that media coverage contributed to creating
the impression that the Internet adoption was more widespread than it
really was, itself creating anxiety about lagging behind (White and Scheb,
2000).[5] In the five-country European qualitative study of the Internet, for

many Dutch interviewees the Net was disappointing and did not live up to expectations. The Dutch researchers in that project pointed out that these people had started out enthusiastically, having heard that the Net was an exciting new medium. Part of their later frustration reflected the fact that they had believed the hype and general media coverage that promised a little too much. If we contrast the Dutch with the Norwegian sample who already had far more (mundane) experience of the Internet through the workplace, the latter often knew what to expect and thus seemed to treat the Internet far more dispassionately (Haddon, 1999a).

Thus media can play a role in showing us how to use ICTs and what they can be useful for. They shape expectations about what is worthwhile and they influence tastes and fashions. But equally, they can create perceptions that do not live up to reality or expectations that are not fulfilled in experience.

Support in Learning to Use the Internet

Obviously there are variations in the degree of complexity of ICTs and hence the difficulty involved in learning how to use them. This is why survey questions asking about sources of support in this process have tended to address the relatively more complex ICTs, such as the PC and more recently the Internet. Such questions are asked less of easier-to-use technologies, like the mobile phone,[6] although of course there are some features where we may well receive advice and tips from others (as when social networks of young people share knowledge about how to get new ringing tones and logos). While these questions deal with support in terms of learning how to achieve something, we can also ask what sources of information we have about when something might be useful (or entertaining) – which might come from social networks, from the media, from experimentation, etc.

The European P-903 survey asked questions about how people learned to use the Internet.[7] It appeared that in a country where there was a low penetration, and generally fewer people with experience of the Internet, it was less easy to draw upon help from family and friends. Instead people were forced to learn how to use the system in more formal settings. By contrast, in countries where Internet penetration was higher, the knowledge was more generally available and it was the more informal sources of information that became more important (Mante-Meijer et al., 2001).

Stages in Early Use

A review of French research on how we learn to use ICTs more generally argued that there were a number of steps between first adoption and the technology becoming more established in our lives. These involved the 'disenchantment' of the technology (i.e. it lost its marvel) and a narrowing of the range of uses compared to the initial exploration phase (Jouet, 2000). While this may seem understandable and familiar, the picture may be a little more complicated, as will become clearer through comparing a number of different studies.

First, this account may not hold true for all groups of people and all ICTs. We can see this in a US study of first-time mobile phone owners who were monitored for six weeks after acquiring their devices (Palen et al., 2001). Many expected that the mobile would be used for limited purposes such as safety or work. But over the period these users discovered more and more circumstances in which the mobile could be useful and so changed their expectations.

The general account of the early career of ICTs was well supported in a French qualitative longitudinal study of the Internet (Lelong and Thomas, 2001).[8] For the majority of users, there was a decrease in usage after a period of initial enthusiastic exploration. This was accompanied by an increase in competence and satisfaction. During the first phase, their searching was erratic, more like surfing, exploring unrelated things whenever they caught the novices' attention. Often the time online passed without them realizing it. The researchers observed that this early stage was then followed by a period in which the users showed more self-discipline and used the Internet more efficiently. Gradually the Internet apprentices learned to interpret better the information from the search engines. They developed a set of tactics to rationalize their navigation and resisted various commercial enticements. As they gained experience, users became more targeted in their approach, sometimes preparing their search strategies before going online. As they anticipated more success, they reduced the number of times they went online and the duration of time online, and they went online at times when the tariff was lower. The Internet was no longer considered a plaything. The Net was used more instrumentally as it became more transparent and familiar (e.g. it was used for acquiring travel tickets, homework, email, etc.). In contrast to the public discourse about a 'revolution' and the Net as an agent of social change, in practice the Internet was incorporated into people's existing habits, scarcely modifying the rhythms or contours of their lives.

If we compare use of the Web and email, the French longitudinal study found that two patterns of usage emerged (Lelong and Thomas, 2001). While the majority attempted to master email, the crucial factor was whether they had a stable social network of people who also used email and who were willing to use it frequently. Some interviewees who lacked this active network abandoned email completely (Lelong and Thomas, 2001). For those with a network of email contacts, using the medium became a ritual habit and going online was an everyday routine, sometimes at a fixed time during the day. In contrast, for those using mainly the Web, going online depended upon the context and was contingent – occurring as and when required, rather than every day. These users did not go online unless there was a specific task. Compared to the former pattern, the French researchers argue that such occasional users were less committed to the Internet, there was less ritualization of use.

The slightly earlier European five-country qualitative study of the Internet found some similar patterns (Haddon, 1999a). In keeping with the French research, for many people usage decreased and the Internet came to play a more limited role in their lives, with the Web being used only on specific occasions or restricted to work purposes. In many households the Internet appeared to be used like teletext, being handy to have at certain times for certain purposes. For some of these users and also for those who used the Web a little more regularly, the pattern was similar to the French study. There was less browsing and more searching. Or else people went to sites that were known to have certain information. Across the countries, email usage became for the majority the part of the Internet that was most routinely and regularly used – although some of this usage was still for work purposes. This was often the function that people were most positive about, involving the electronic extension of a familiar practice: checking for mail (Haddon, 1999a).

However, the first stage of excitement did not necessarily happen in the home at all. For example, few Norwegian participants reported early enthusiasm and experimenting when they first subscribed at home because so many of the sample had already had their initial experience of the Net at work. The Internet was already more mundane by then and they tended to carry over into the home the patterns of use established in the workplace.

After this early exploratory phase there were always a certain number of interviewees, across the countries, for whom there was still some pleasure to be had in exploring the Internet (or more rarely chatting online or playing online games). These people, who were not necessarily computer enthusiasts nor indeed just males, set aside time for such usage. Searching, for example, could easily slip into browsing if something interesting caught the user's attention. For some interviewees, then, relaxing on the Internet could be an alternative to relaxing in front of the television or reading a newspaper. In yet other cases, usage had steadily grown, and continued to grow.[9] For example, they used email more and more as people they knew also gained Internet access. Some reported that they were planning their own website (as self-employed teleworkers) or had recently tried downloading software or electronic transactions.

If we now look to the North America experience, the context is immediately different. Higher adoption rates were always likely to make email more attractive precisely because of the point made above: compared to many European countries an individual is more likely to have people they can contact online. In a US quantitative study, a sample first surveyed in 2001 and reinterviewed in 2002 consisted of people with different levels of experience (Horrigan and Rainie, 2002a). Looking at the change between interviews, some findings were similar to the European ones. Use became more serious and functional. However, the participants in this study did more kinds of things online as they gained experience (rather than narrowing their interests), even though they spent a little less time on the Net. In that sense, the researchers argued, the Internet had become woven into people's daily lives more. They too described how, with experience, the Internet seemed to lose excitement. Yet users still valued it as much as before, or more than ever. The complexity of the changes can be shown in the case of email. After a year has passed, users were less likely to email family members on a daily basis. However, more sent emails to family and friends about serious subjects such as sharing worries and asking for advice.

Learning to Use the Internet

The authors of the French Internet study outlined how, in general, the literature on the nature of expertise characterized technical know-how. This knowledge was often tacit, uncodifed and passed on from person to person rather than being explained in documentation (Lelong and Thomas, 2001). The researchers argued that knowledge of the Internet was similar. Users found it difficult to put their expertise into words, to describe in detail their newfound abilities.

Yet at the same time, all of those interviewed stressed the necessity of intensive and prolonged practice, the laboriousness of acquiring competence and the investment that it required. They evoked the metaphors of work and school, of being systematic, of persevering, of working as hard as possible – often mentioning that this was a solo effort, involving time alone using the Net. To progress it was necessary to stop relying on manuals, on hotlines, on friends you could call up by phone. Instead it was important to develop one's own competence in order to cope with difficulties and not depend on others – to be autonomous (Lelong and Thomas, 2001).[10]

A slightly different image emerges in a Canadian longitudinal study of Quebec teenagers. Although the adolescents learned to use the Internet very quickly, the knowledge of the majority remained basic. These users did not look into the full potentialities of the technology (Millerand et al., 1999). The teenagers learnt the minimum in order to surf and to chat and did not invest time in learning more about navigation aids, for example. They had only a vague idea of the architecture of the network, but that did not prevent them from using it. It did not matter to them if they were not sure how they had reached a certain site. The pleasure of discovery was enough. The researchers observed that usually it was family and friends who first taught them the rudiments of navigation – in contrast to working through manuals.

This picture fits in with the findings of the more wide-ranging review of French research on ICTs. It argued that normally only a minority of users invest heavily in their ICTs, such as Internet enthusiasts (Jouet, 2000). The majority are content to master only some of the functions (e.g. only a few of those offered by the software). Nevertheless, the studies reviewed generally suggested that this minimal exploration was often enough to provide sufficient satisfaction in proportion to the effort invested.

Locating ICTs in the Home

Where ICTs are located in the home is important because it can have a bearing on use. However, finding a space for technology is not merely a question of finding 'room' – it reflects family ideologies (Silverstone et al., 1992; Silverstone and Haddon, 1996b; Ling and Thrane, 2001).

In Chapter 3, we saw that parents often put the computer in a place where they could monitor their children's use. In Chapter 4, the decision about where to locate the phone was once again used as a strategy for controlling the technology. But using location to restrict use is not the only consideration. Especially when there are several children in a household, decisions about location can reflect attempts to share resources in the home. One US study observed that this was a key reason for locating the PC in a public space within the home (e.g. dining room, family room, spare room) or else in a semi-private one such as the study (Frohlich and Kraut, 2003). In a similar spirit, a Norwegian study found that people sometimes placed the computer in the parents' bedroom since it was regarded a more neutral terrain in the home compared to one of the children's bedrooms (Ling and Thrane, 2001).

Some decisions about location actually attempted to broaden ICT access and usage. French researchers studied experiments that provided people with new terminals to access the Internet. They observed that in the homes that already had Internet access via a PC, the participants had initially imagined that the new terminals would somehow collectivize Internet usage – where the Net had previously been the domain of one family member (Lelong and Beaudouin, 2001). It was because of this aspiration that they often placed the new terminals in communal rooms (e.g. the living room, dining room).

Even if ICTs like the computer find a physical place in the home, this can still create problems. For example, locating PCs in public spaces within the home can lead to problems such as a lack of privacy and affect the user's ability to concentrate (Frohlich and Kraut, 2003). Sometimes the presence of the technology may also come into conflict with some of the values associated with home life. For example, the Norwegian researchers pointed out just how difficult it was to choose a place to put the PC in many households (Ling and Thrane, 2001). The living room was sometimes felt to be inappropriate because the computer represented work. This clashed with the type of place that the living room was supposed to be. Interviewees also talked of the noisy fan in the PC, the ugly appearance of the machine and the fact that it generated paper and other clutter. So even when the computer was reluctantly allowed into the living room, it was sometimes camouflaged by visual barriers or located in back corners.[11] In the long run, the researchers thought that there was potential for perceptions to change over time. The authors referred back to related Norwegian discussions when TV sets were first introduced in the 1950 and 1960s. At that time television itself broke with the previous conventions whereby the living room was supposed to be a place reserved for reading and conversation.[12]

Lastly, some decisions about the location and use of ICTs are affected by household members' desire to manage the impression they give to the outside world, to manage display (Silverstone et al., 1992; Silverstone and Haddon, 1996b). This was particularly clear in a British qualitative study of telework and ICTs in the early 1990s, as described in Chapter 8.

The Influence of Existing Practices on the Consumption of New ICTs

When assessing how much the Information Society is 'revolutionary', critics have questioned the speed and scale of change, Another approach has been to ask to what extent new innovations develop from what already exists and therefore to what extent change is really 'evolutionary'. For example, in many senses television built upon programming practices established by radio (Winston, 1989), and radio itself originally drew up practices from, for example, vaudeville.

But if the very form that ICTs take builds upon predecessors then this is itself relevant for understanding their later consumption. For example, the action genre of video games was in part derived from the game-play of pinball. In fact, video games machines were first introduced into arcades as a replacement for pinball, (Haddon, 1999c). In which case, we can appreciate why the practices of (especially) young males collectively competing to get the highest scores in interactive games, watching others play and learning tactics themselves derived in large part from the games' origin in pinball.

People build upon past experiences when faced with new ICTs. This point was emphasized in the review of French research, whose author referred to the longer term collective construction of use. Uses of ICTs are always inserted into family and work practices that pre-exist or are already under construction. The adoption of ICTs takes place against a backdrop of preceding techniques and practices, and new uses are often an extension of what has gone before (Jouet, 2000).

This can be illustrated in a Canadian study of Internet use by Quebec teenagers. The research first pointed out how these adolescents visited websites that were related to their pre-existing interests (e.g. in sport, TV, music, cinema, etc.) (Millerand et al., 1999). The researchers then discussed the sociability patterns of this age group – how, for example, these young people liked to chat among their friends. This practice carried over into Internet use. Friends sitting in the same room full of computers would talk to each other or else they would chat while standing together looking at a screen. The teenagers also preferred the online chat function compared to email because it enabled immediate chatting, like the telephone (Millerand et al., 1999). As regards the mobile phone, various researchers have commented on the fact that some modern usages reflect older interests. For example sending secret text messages and mobile email in the classroom is an updated, and less visible, version of passing paper notes around without the teacher seeing (Ling and Yttri, 2002, for Norway; Ito and Daisuke, 2003, for Japan).

What we learn to do with one technology can affect our evaluation (and take-up) of another. For instance, in the French study of new terminals for accessing the Internet (e.g. web-phones, web-TV) the researchers argued that existing users had learnt to do some things online precisely because their original access had been via the PC interface. This meant that it was actually a disadvantage to use certain alternative terminals if they did not allow the practices that relied upon having a hard disk available with utility programs, using a mouse or other pointing system, typing on a keyboard, etc. On some of these alternative terminals the screen was perceived as being too small (relative to the computer), the keyboard was seen as non-standard (compared to the computer), and email could not be saved or printed. All of this led to some frustration (Lelong and Beaudouin, 2001). The point is that for PC users, the computer was the reference point against which all other alternatives were judged – and found wanting.

The Influence of New ICTs on Consumption and on Existing Technologies

To what extent do the newly adopted technologies compete with or complement older ICTs? Historical examples might include the effects of television watching on cinema going and radio listening. These latter declined significantly, an effect that has been explained by the 'functional equivalence' of these different options (Robinson et al., 2002). Yet other analysts have pointed out that the picture is not so straightforward. The influence of TV's arrival was not just one of decreasing the time spent going to the cinema and listening to radio. The experience of these other media changed, as their use became more specialized (Johnsson-Smaragdi, 2001, on radio). This author observed that at a societal level old media are rarely completely displaced, in contrast to the level of the individual where particular people may give up some ICTs.

Later examples of a certain amount of displacement might include the way newly arriving TV channels, including those of satellite, have influenced how much time people spend watching the existing terrestrial ones. In the communications field, the equivalent question we might want to ask is about the extent to which mobile telephony and email might have had any effect on our use of the fixed-line phone.

The review of French research on ICTs in general came to the conclusion that new innovations often complement the older ones. For example, video games did not substitute for the TV, nor has electronic messaging displaced the telephone. But these new ICTs lead us to use pre-existing objects in new ways and in general increase the complexity of our media and communication practices (Jouet, 2000). This sometimes means that the use of all media is adjusted (Bolter and Grushin (1999), cited in Livingstone, 2003).

A British longitudinal survey would provide some support for this conclusion about complementarity in the case of telecoms.[13] First, it showed that only about a quarter of those surveyed thought that email made no significant difference to their use of the traditional phone. The remainder were equally divided between whether the impact of email was large or small (Haddon, 2000c). In the five-country European qualitative study, email usually complemented fixed-line telephony, not only for social messaging but also when interviewees sought information. People with the Internet still found times when they preferred to ask for information over the phone. The main exception was in the case of international calls, where cheap (or cost-free if made from work) emails sometimes replaced expensive calls to other countries. Or they led to more communication with people abroad than would have taken place in the past. For those few who had fax machines, some faxes had been displaced by email. But even the fax machine remained a complementary technology when people wanted to send a text that was available only in hard copy form. For some, email had replaced letter writing to those friends who were seen less regularly.

French research on early mobile phone use suggested that when people want to make longer social calls they often still used the traditional phone (De Gournay et al., 1997). The British longitudinal survey conducted at the end of the twentieth century also showed that people did not think that the mobile phone was substituting for traditional telephony to the same extent as email. Nearly four-fifths thought that the mobile phone had made hardly an impact on their use of the fixed line. This suggests that for the vast majority of people mobile calls complemented traditional phone use rather than replacing them – i.e. the mobile calls were additional, for whatever reason. The other implication is that while the mobile phone allowed people to replace fixed-line calls in terms of time-shifting certain calls to more convenient moments, these statistics suggested that this was not a major practice adopted by the majority – at that time (Haddon, 2000c). The UK, like other countries, has seen an increasing proliferation of mobile phone tariffs, making some calls effectively 'free' (free minutes per month, free calls to people using the same operator etc.). Fixed-line providers have started to offer flat-rate fees, per month. It remains to be seen how much effect these changes will have on the current pattern of calls

When we turn to the relation between Internet use and TV viewing, the quantitative evidence is mixed. This may in part reflect methodological considerations.[14] In a US study in which people were interviewed in 2001 and reinterviewed in 2002, a quarter claimed that the Internet had led to a decrease in the time spent watching TV (Horrigan and Rainie, 2002a). Some cross-sectional surveys have also found this relationship (Nie and Erbring, 2002). On the other hand, other US analyses, of more than one dataset, suggest that Internet use has not led to less television viewing overall (Cole and Robinson, 2002; Neustadtl and Robinson, 2002; Robinson et al., 2002), a point also made in a UK longitudinal study (Anderson and Tracey, 2001, 2002).[15]

We might at least get some clues about the detailed processes at work from the five-country European qualitative study on the Internet. A number of interviewees reported that they had switched from watching some television programmes to using the Internet at certain times. But these particular people tended to have less interest in television generally, or else this switch to the Internet happened at those times of the day when they had a low commitment to watching TV (Haddon, 1999a). However, the Internet could not displace television at times when, for example, there was a stronger commitment to particular programmes (e.g. the news) or where TV watching counted as family time (e.g. watching in couples or with children). The Internet could not so easily displace television watching when the latter was perceived as 'resting time'. This might be after work or late in the evenings when fatigue had set in and a less demanding activity was desired. As regards information from the TV, the UK research found that while the Internet had occasionally led to some decline in teletext use, for the most part the technologies were complementary and teletext continued to be used (e.g. for weather, TV listings, holidays, etc.)

Finally, in the Québec research, the Internet did not, on the whole, lead teenagers to change their evaluation of, or practices relating to, traditional media such as television and radio. The exceptions were that some of the more intensive users now played fewer video games and watched less TV. However, quite a number did comment on the fact that the Internet allowed them more freedom than television, whose choices were in the form of fixed programmes. Nevertheless, the Internet did not simply displace all television watching – the teenagers often went online after watching the TV programmes that they liked (Millerand et al., 1999).

We need to be sensitive not only to any shifts in the use of existing ICTs brought about by the arrival of new innovations but also to the new issues within households which they raise. For example, in British research on ICTs in homes conducted during the early 1990s, some of the participants reported new conflicts between parents and children over access to the TV once video games consoles entered the home. By requiring the TV screen for display, games competed with broadcast programmes (Haddon and Silverstone, 1994). If we take a slightly older example, in the early to mid-1980s, early British home computers utilized the TV screen as a monitor. One domestic consequence of this development was the transfer of any second TV sets to the children's bedrooms (e.g. TVs that used to be based in the kitchen and which could be watched during meals or while cooking took place). While these early games and computers provided the justification for granting children access to these second TV sets, those children could then watch television programmes in private. In some households this was the first time that this had been allowed (Haddon and Silverstone, 1994).

Longer Term Careers of ICTs

US analysts have drawn attention to how the 'shifting environment' in which ICTs exist can influence patterns of use (Cummings and Kraut, 2002). As evidence of this, the researchers compared responses from identical people in 1995 and then again in 1996. People's use had altered even over this short period. In the first survey the Internet was used more for work than pleasure. By the time of the second survey, this difference had vanished.[16]

This environment referred to by these analysts could include changes in mass media coverage, as in the case of increased references to email in news articles, in popular films and in cartoons. It could include what other people do. The fact that more people went online made email an even more attractive function. And it could include the preferences and expectations of other people, as when friends made comments about emailing each other: 'As a community of users appropriates an innovation, they develop and communicate norms about acceptable use, which can influence the behaviour of peers and subsequent generations' (Cummings and Kraut, 2002, p. 224).

In addition to changing representations and wider patterns of consumption, part of that shifting environment consists of changes related to the technology itself. These analysts cited the arrival of new services on the Internet, some of which had emerged as companies themselves responded to changes in the user base and motivations. For example, the development of instant messaging and 'buddy lists' made the Internet more attractive for interpersonal communication. Meanwhile 'high-speed networks make it more appropriate for transporting bandwidth entertainment applications' (p. 223) such as downloading music files and playing graphics-filled games.

We can see a similar process in British research during the mid-1990s. This revealed how new telephone services had had a bearing on the way the basic fixed phone was used (Haddon, 1997a). For instance, some of the young elderly remembered when it first became possible to order by credit card over the phone. Their subsequent usage of the phone increased once they got into the habit of buying various goods and services in this way. The 1980s and 1990s saw an increase in technical helplines, social support lines (e.g. the Samaritans), chatlines as well as radio phone-ins and the promotion by TV companies of competitions where the audience is invited to phone in with answers – at premium phone prices.

Such additions not only affected phone usage, but also influenced the whole way in which the phone was managed in some households. For example, fears of teenagers running up huge bills on chatlines, or indeed accessing sexlines, led to anxiety and domestic conflicts. Radio phone-ins required new forms of negotiation. Some parents limited the extent to which their children could take part in such competitions because of the implications for the phone bill. Of course, the Internet has itself given the phone a new role. It has led to similar concerns about costs, about blocking the phone line and about what can be accessed from the home, and it has led to new ways of managing the use of the phone for going online (Haddon, 1999a).

What about other changes in the nature of ICTs? Research has shown how changes in the quality of connections, the use of new types of terminal as well as speed and tariff changes can all affect consumption. For example, a French study of experiments using ADSL found that broadband led to more diverse and more sophisticated use. People played more online, took part in forums and discussions, downloaded more files, made more use of multimedia and constructed more personal web-pages. The high speed allowed greater fluidity in navigation, and so enabled people to more explore more complex functionalities. The researchers argued that the rapid response enabled by faster transmission speeds facilitated trial and error learning and that the flat rate of payment associated with these new forms of access removed worries about the cost of learning. So other people besides the main 'expert' in the household could learn to use the Internet (Lelong and Beaudouin, 2001).

If we consider the wider or public history of the mobile phone, in its relatively short life as a mass market product it has already evolved in certain respects. There are of course the changes in design, most visibly in its shrinkage in size and presentation as a fashion object. In terms of functionality, we saw how the addition of text messaging had important implications for its use by youth. Changes in marketing in terms of the addition of prepayment cards had a bearing on how the phone was managed within household relationships (Ling and Helmersen, 2000). We have already noted the proliferation of tariffs.

It is not just the arrival of totally new innovations that makes a difference to the usage and management of ICTs in the home. The multiplication of already familiar technologies is also a factor. For example, having extra telephone handsets in private spaces such as bedrooms enabled more privacy for individuals when they made calls from home (Haddon, 1997a). The British teleworking study showed that when a teleworker upgraded the computer it often meant that partners of teleworkers and their children could now have easier access to the old PC. While this led to a change in the career of those particular old computers, it also had implications in terms of the computer's general place in the home. It reduced conflicts arising from different people wanting to use the machine at the same time. Finally, there is the case of the second TV set. The arrival of a new TV set not only means a potentially new role for the old set, but also can change the experience of viewing, reducing communal TV watching – and hence 'family time together' – as on occasion some household members retired to another room to watch the particular programmes they wanted to see on the old TV set (Haddon and Silverstone, 1994).

Conclusions

To sum up, wider social discourses in general and media coverage in particular can have a role in influencing the reception of ICTs. They help to create interest, even enthusiasm, but they also shape expectations. Media, sometimes at the instigation of companies, can also act as part of the shifting environment in which technologies are located, presenting new representations of those technologies. This serves to underline a key theme of this book, the importance of examining the various social contexts in which individuals act in order to understand their experience of ICTs.

One such context is our experience of existing technologies, since these can affect our relationship to newer ICTs. This makes it all the more important to consider the whole media and communications picture, the interrelation between new and old ICTs, rather than evaluating each element in isolation. Conversely, the arrival of new ICTs can alter our relationships with the ICTs that we already use, although it appears to be only rarely that one completely displaces the other. More commonly, as our repertoire of options expands, we readjust our practices.

Domestication analysis initially focused on early career of ICTs, especially the period before and immediately after adoption. But it did so in terms of specifying a range of general processes such as ICT use finding a place in people's time structures. If we want to examine the early careers of specific technologies, then we have to take into account their particular nature, including such matters as what one can do with them. Using the worked example of Internet use, we saw how it was possible to examine a range of developments during this early stage. These included changes in the purpose for which the Net was used, the range of uses, the manner in which it was used, the timing and circumstances of use, the degree to which it was valued or found to be exciting and the way and extent to which expertise developed. Moreover, some these studies showed the variety of technological careers that could emerge for different individuals and in different households.

While early domestication work had outlined the general processes by which ICTs find a physical and symbolic space in the home, subsequent empirical work has provided far more detail of the particular factors at work. We have seen that the decision as to where to locate ICTs can be used as a strategy either for limiting use or for promoting access. It can be a way of managing the impressions we give to others. But that process of location is also shaped by the values associated with domestic spaces. This create dilemmas, unease and attempts to alter the visual impact of ICTs in these spaces.

Finally, although the early domestication literature said relatively less about the period after that early career, in this chapter we have seen some of the factors that have a bearing on our longer term experience of ICTs. These include the wider adoption of these technologies and the changing norms about use, new public representations of technologies, developments in nature of the ICTs themselves, the arrival of complementary or competing technologies and services and even the sheer multiplication of existing technologies. These can all alter our relationships to ICTs, not only in terms of patterns of usage but also in terms of how we experience and have to socially manage them.

Notes

1. Here we have a sharp contrast with the mobile phone, which was never included in these discourses and which never had the symbolic prominence of the Internet, despite being successful in the marketplace.
2. The process of feminization was also noted in Norwegian research on changing mobile phone advertisements and images of gender (Bakke, 1997).
3. Media coverage is not, however, monolithic. One study of three journals in Germany showed some differences in their representation of the Internet (Rössler, 2001).
4. The way in which such representations work, associating symbolic values with mobile phones, has been explored more systematically in a study of non-promotional Chinese print media in Hong Kong (Yung, 2003).
5. The researchers reported a survey showing that two-thirds of those interviewed, including users, overestimated the level of adoption and thought of themselves as lagging behind others.
6. One early US trial conducted in 1993 allowed participants to use mobiles before they were widespread. This showed up some of the difficulties that users faced even with technology that in many ways resembled the familiar phone. Examples of difficulties included figuring out the need to end the call when hanging up, working out how to set up and obtain access to voice mail, navigating menus and clearing the display when making a dialling error (Gant and Kiesler, 2001). Even by 2001,

another US study was showing that some confusions still existed as regards mobile phone features and billing (Palen et al., 2001). It would appear that problems and misunderstandings relating to mobile use were covered less in European research. Since the mobile markets were generally becoming more established in Europe, different questions have dominated research agendas.

7. For example, the P-903 research found that across the European sample the largest portion of the Internet users had initially been helped out by a school or work colleague (29 per cent), 25 per cent were helped by a friend or partner and 25 per cent found out for themselves with or without manuals. Only 1 per cent had used a helpline. There were differences between the nine countries. In some countries with lower diffusion rates, use was often associated with institutional settings, i.e. at work, at school or at university. Almost half of the Internet users from the Czech Republic had learned to use the Internet from a school or work colleague, while in the other countries this percentage was much lower, between 21 per cent and 33 per cent.

8. This study involved interviews with thirty people four months after they first gained access to the Internet. They were reinterviewed after a year.

9. This general point that usage can change in a variety of ways, sometimes decreasing, sometimes increasing, was also made about computer use in an Australian study (Lally, 2002). As in the Internet study, Lally found that while for many people the 'novelty effect' of computer use wore off, for others some of the excitement remained.

10. However, in the five-country study of the Internet there were examples of people who were willing at times to turn to outsiders for particular forms of help even after they had mastered the basics of the Internet.

11. In an Australian study, within a broader discussion of how computers found a place within the ensemble of objects in the home, Lally discussed how the home computer was made to fit in with the aesthetics of the household, for example, by having computer covers made with a fabric to match the decor of the room (Lally, 2002).

12. The authors also pointed out that the TV set was only just starting to be established in Norwegain kitchens. In fact, for many Norwegians it still does not fit in there. There is a trend towards having a large kitchen as a space for the family to meet up together and hence the TV's arrival is a threat to this goal. For some the kitchen remains a TV-free zone, for others it is allowed in but only if it is a small set, while yet other households allow only certain viewing in the kitchen, e.g. the news.

13. Data from the 1996 Telsoc five-country survey showed the users of mobiles were actually heavier uses of the fixed line. This does not prove a causal link, but it does suggest that substitution was not taking place (Fortunati, 2001).

14. Robinson and Godbey (1999, p. 156) discussed the difficulty faced in 'trying to estimate the complex effects of a new technology on their lives' and therefore favoured a survey reporting what people did yesterday. Although they initially found that more computer use correlated to less TV viewing, on deeper analysis this result could be explained away by the influence of social class (people from higher social classes watched less TV and were more likely to be computer users). When the researchers looked specifically at Internet users, their TV viewing was not much different from the rest of the population.

15. The authors observed that if use of the Internet takes time away from other activities, it might do so by adjusting small amounts of the time to spend on a range of activities. This argument was reinforced by the replies from the qualitative component of this study, in which people could often not pinpoint exactly what the time spent using the Internet had displaced.

16. Cummings and Kraut (2002) acknowledged the fact that they managed only weak results but observed that this was a small sample examined over only a short period.

10

Conclusions

Each of the chapters in this book has signposted key methodological or conceptual issues, identified gaps in approaches and indicated the scope for further lines of analysis. The conclusion now reflects upon the core framework of domestication that has shaped this introductory text. It then considers the implications of the issues raised for those involved in companies researching and designing ICTs and for students entering this field of study. Lastly, it considers how we might go about evaluating the social consequences of ICTs – as a worked example for students to think about how this material might be used.[1]

The Domestication Framework

The introduction indicated that the domestication framework provided the main springboard for thinking through the various chapters. This influenced the examples drawn upon, some of the agendas of interest in this book and many of its organizing principles. In this sense, readers entering this field of study need to be aware that there are no neutral introductory texts. That includes this one.

That said, this book has attempted to address related agendas and make connections with other traditions of research, even if the researchers concerned would not necessarily see themselves as operating within the domestication framework. These related areas include various studies from communications research, studies of social networks, traditions particularly focused on the process of learning to use ICTs or becoming a user, work on gift relationships and research on the experience of time. Some literatures can complement and inform the type of micro-social analysis associated with domestication, such as the wider societal social construction of parenthood and childhood.

The domestication framework has served to sensitize researchers to some of the processes at work in incorporating ICTs into everyday life. It has been employed outside of academic contexts. A number of the studies cited throughout this book were sponsored by companies. Chapter 2 on uneven adoption indicated how this framework could be relevant to those operating in the field of policy. While methodologically associated with qualitative research, Chapter 4 on managing relationships showed how the interests of the framework could be translated into quantitative studies.

Chapters 7 and 5 on mobility and social networks both indicated ways in which there remains scope for expanding the areas where ideas from domestication could be applied. In the case of mobility, this meant looking outside the home to deal with certain facets of portable technologies, ICT-related interaction in public spaces and emerging agendas on mobility. In the case of social networks, this involved looking beyond the interactions of household members to consider interactions with others beyond the household and ask what equivalent process of domestication may exist within such collectivities.

This raises the question of whether one can start to go further than considering known members of social networks to talk about domestication processes among certain sections of society. Or, indeed, to talk about domestication by society itself – as some writers have done. Maybe. But then it is important to remember the original context in which domestication was formulated. In the introduction we saw how that early work provided a general framework for processes such as how ICTs are fitted into the time and space structures of the home, or rather, of different homes. What would the equivalent processes be at a societal level?

The more problematic question or claim that one sometimes encounters concerns whether a particular technology or service has 'been domesticated' in society. If there is a lesson to be learnt from the micro-social analyses described in Chapters 8 and 9 on changing life circumstances and the careers of ICTs, it is that we are dealing with a dynamic process. This should make us wary of saying that an end-state has finally been reached. We can always question the degree to which ICTs are integrated into our lives and ask how much scope there is for that to change.

Implications for Product Developers

The growth of interest shown by ICT companies in researching this field was outlined in the introduction. We saw that quite a number of the studies cited in this book were financed in part or in whole by companies developing these technologies. Many of the European studies came from social scientists specifically working within or on behalf of telecom companies. In addition, many design and engineering students, some of whom might one day work on the development of ICTs, now have a social science input within their courses. Since both the company researchers and students of ICTs are intended audiences for this book, it is worth making some specific final observations for these communities.

For those readers starting out in the ICT industries, this book has emphasized the merits of considering not only individuals as potential users of technologies, but also various aspects of the social contexts in which they operate. People do not just use ICTs but they also manage them, largely because they are interacting with others. We have seen the various ways in which this interaction shapes the experience of ICTs, whether it is interaction in the household, or among wider social networks. We have seen how it influences the very interest that people take in some technologies in the first place, their ability to use them, the time available for using ICTs, and indeed the particular usages and practices that emerge.

How does this translate into a practical guide for product and service developers, be that in market research, various levels and types of design, product presentation, pricing, deciding routes to market, etc.? It means looking beyond anticipated users to be aware of gatekeepers. They may or may not use technologies themselves, but how might they shape the access and usage of others? It means asking how usage, or particular forms of usage, is going to be socially supported. In this respect, what are the difficulties faced by particular groups when acquiring and using ICTs and in what ways can the developers help to overcome these?

We have seen how it is important to be aware that ICTs are always symbolic. Over and above the images offered by their developers and providers, ICTs can have perceived potential consequences for social life. They can offer the promise of a better future or pose a threat. The latter has been shown in concerns about the effects of the Internet on our sociability and about the consequences of TV for the balance in our lives. More generally, these are worries about what type of people ICTs will make or entice us to become. So whether people's reactions are positive, negative or ambiguous, one question for developers is how and why technologies and services take on specific meanings?

The take-up of new ICTs is influenced in part by the experience of what has gone before. What will the relation of new ICTs be to existing ones? In what way do they involve building on past practices? How do they change our relationships to and use of older technologies? In other words, how will the arrival of new ICTs change the way we manage our ensemble of ICTs, or our range of communications options?

How would knowing the history of past innovations (and which past innovations) affect forecasts of whether and how adoption of new ICTs might change over time? When forecasting the usage of particular products and services, what constraints on use do product developers believe that people face, in terms of time as well as other factors? What can be learnt from non-adopters and dropouts, whose actions question the product and the role it can play in their lives? What issues and problems does the arrival of new ICTs in people's lives raise?

When trying to chart markets, what social process are at work behind the construction of any particular adoption and usage figures? In other words, what are they including and excluding? What behaviours should we consider examining to understand more fully what ICTs mean in people's lives, what role they are playing and how integrated they are into people's routines?

The chapters that have gone before aim to sensitize product developers to the elements that might be considered in developing and answering such questions. One way to actively engage with this material is to develop this checklist of questions further, or to ask how the various studies cited across the chapters answer these questions. These chapters provide specific examples as well as some general guidelines about where to look, what questions to ask and what frameworks could be useful. Nevertheless, those developing ICTs still need to apply these in their particular areas of innovation.

Research on the social shaping of ICTs has already shown how those developing products often act like 'detectives', looking for evidence when mounting business cases (Cawson et al., 1995; Haddon, 2002). The examples discussed in this book should help to enhance that process.

Implications for Students

Turning to the student readership, obviously some of the questions they would want to ask would overlap with those of interest to ICT developers. But often students are required to stand further back from particular products to think of broader issues. Examples of the types of questions I have posed during the course of my own teaching include how ICTs are 'gendered', how they are symbolic and with what consequences, how and why popular concerns about these technologies and services emerge, whether we should talk about an information revolution, or how ICTs influence our experience of time and space.

Such broad questions certainly require an appreciation of various histories, although product developers would benefit from being aware of these as well. This can mean being sensitive to the wider social and historical construction of experience in order to help us to make sense of why certain patterns, certain behaviours, exist at a particular point in time (or a particular culture).

It can include knowing how past innovations were socially shaped, their patterns of adoption and use, the micro-social issues arising from this as well as the broader social consequences. It can also require us to know how past biographical experiences, as well as past technological ones, have had a bearing upon the way different groups react to contemporary innovations.

These are not the only important histories. Others of relevance include the influence of wider discourses in general and media in particular on our hopes and expectations of ICTs – as well as our concerns about them. They include the history of debates, such as the policy interest in social exclusion. This in turn means being aware of the history of concepts, the terms of debates and the assumptions they make. And they include the history of social science frameworks and methodologies utilized to making sense of and investigate ICTs – as well as their related critiques. If the product developer is a certain type of detective, so too is the student in this field, but often emphasizing different types of evidence to address different levels of inquiry.

The Social Consequences of ICTs: A Worked Example

This last section aims to show how students might use the material from this book to address the types of questions posed earlier. The example considered here is how we might evaluate the social consequences of ICTs. The question can be addressed in more than one way, at more than one level, and arriving at different overall conclusions depending on what types of evidence and argument are emphasized.

One possible starting point is to ask why this is an important question. For example, this book has referred to, and at various points addressed, a number of debates about the potential, or feared, social consequences of ICTs. This can be seen, for example, in the discussions of the digital divide, concerns about children and ICTs, fears about ICTs affecting the time we spend with family and friends, or influencing the balance of time we spend on different activities. When faced with such concerns, one has to ask a number of questions. Why are these important issues and what factors have shaped these fears? What assumptions do they make, what conceptions (e.g. of children) are they based upon, what values do they reflect? Ultimately, one needs to appreciate the history of predictions or of apprehensions (e.g. about addiction to technology) and know where they have been made manifest in the past. Of course, understanding the basis and origin of claims about social consequences is only a first step. Sometimes serious methodological issues are involved in researching them, and there is scope for discussing the issues involved in the way we evaluate these consequences.

Apart from these more general observations, at another level one could discuss particular ICTs and specific social consequences. For example, Canadian researchers summarized three different overall positions regarding the anticipated effects of the Internet on sociability and social capital (Wellman et al., 2001). These were a utopian viewpoint where the Internet increased social capital (to use one of the terms from these discussions), a dystopian analysis where it decreased social capital and an approach where the Internet was seen to supplement social capital (Wellman et al., 2001; see also Katz et al., 2001 and Katz and Rice, 2002b, who outline related 'optimistic' and 'pessimistic' perspectives). Of course, putting all possible viewpoints, some more nuanced, into just three camps might be seen as setting up strawmen. However, such divisions as these can nevertheless provide a base for making some general observations, over and above the particular case of the Internet and social capital. In this instance, the authors favoured the third option, albeit acknowledging here and elsewhere the complexity of factors at work (e.g. Wellman and Haythornthtwaite, 2002). They argued that the Internet was simply not so influential on our lives as was claimed in the other two options. The authors questioned how fundamentally the Internet changed our social relations one way or another, with the Internet being seen as just one tool among others through which we organize our everyday life.[2]

It is possible to use the material in this book to discuss ways in which ICTs might have brought about some change, where they might have made some difference to everyday life. For example, this was captured in the discussions of changes in the ability of parents to monitor children's use of ICTs, reflecting in part children's ability to use technologies such as mobile phones to avoid surveillance when they want to. We saw the new ways in which we use ICTs to keep in touch with, manage and even meet up with social networks. This involved new ways of using ICTs to organize time and mobility. We saw how ICTs can also have diverse effect on the very experience of time (e.g. contributing to a sense of pressure as well as serving to alleviate such pressures) and of mobility (e.g. in terms of being 'away' from home). Just managing those ICTs can have consequences for daily social life, as manifested in people's behaviour in public spaces that relate to mobile phone use. In other words, we do see instances of new practices. This would be understandable because we know historically that some behaviour changes over time through the arrival of ICTs (as happened with the adoption of basic telephone and broadcast media). Sometimes, researchers have mobilized the available evidence to make the case that some of the changes brought about by ICTs like the Internet are, on balance, to the good (e.g. Katz and Rice, 2002b).

That said, one reason for being wary of arguments that ICTs might produce more major changes in the short term is our awareness of the range of social factors creating a degree of inertia. At various points this book has outlined the social constraints on the way ICTs are taken up or operate in our lives. These include our economic circumstances, our personal time commitments and the broader time structures in which we operate, as well as the expectations of our social networks and of those co-present others in public spaces. The case of the young elderly showed that the historical experiences of different generations can also create some resistance to ICTs. Ultimately we also have to be aware that, with varying degrees of success, people do try to manage ICTs. They reflect upon the influence that ICTs already have or might have upon their lives and they try to control them. This was made manifest in people's strategies to regulate the use of ICTs, for example, parents' attempts to influence children's use and to control communications. To come back to the types of general positions outlined earlier, it is these types of considerations that makes one wonder whether, at least in the shorter term, any social consequences of ICTs will turn out to be far more modest than those leaning towards utopian or dystopian positions might have predicted.

Notes

1. It has not been possible to discuss all social change and consequences within the framework of this book. For example, it has been noted by several authors that we, literally, communicate more. For example, a French study estimated that between 1990 and 2000 communications by French people increased fivefold; the main cause of this was extra textual communications such as text messaging and email (Rivère and Licoppe, 2003). This and other studies underline the fact that we are having to manage an increasingly complex communications repertoire. A similar point has been made about youth and screen-based media (Livingstone and Bovill, 2001b; Livingstone, 2002).
2. This would find a sympathetic ear among many European researchers, which implies being wary of how strong, or how revolutionary, any social consequences are likely to be.

Bibliography

Adams, J. (2000), 'Hypermobility', *Prospect*, March, http://www.prospect-magazine. co.uk/highlights/hypermobility/index.htlm.

Anderson, B. (ed.) (2001), *e-living: State of the Art Review*, Martlesham: BTexact Technologies, UK.

——and Tracey, K. (2001), 'Digital Living: The Impact (or Otherwise) of the Internet on Everyday Life', *American Behavioral Scientist*, 45(3): 456–75.

——and Tracey, K. (2002), 'Digital Living: The Impact (or Otherwise) of the Internet on Everyday Life', in Wellman, B. and Haythornthwaite, C. (eds) *The Internet in Everyday Life*, Oxford: Blackwell.

——Gale, C., Gower, A., France, E., Jones, M., Lacohee, H., McWilliam, A., Tracey, K. and Trimby, M. (2002), 'Digital Living – People-Centred Innovation and Strategy', *BT Technology Journal*, 20(2): 11–29.

Ariès, P. (1973), *Centuries of Childhood*, Harmondsworth: Penguin.

Bakardjieva, M. (2001), 'Becoming a Domestic Internet User', paper for the conference *e-Usages*, Paris, 12–14 June.

——and Smith, R. (2001), 'The Internet in Everyday Life: Computer Networking from the Standpoint of the Domestic User', *New Media and Society*, 3(1): 67–84.

Bakke, J. (1997), 'Competition in Mobile telephony and Images of Communication', in Frissen, V. (ed.) *Proceedings from COSTA4 Granite Workshop Gender, ITCs and Everyday Life: Mutual Shaping Processes*, Amsterdam, 8–11 February, 6, Brussels: COSTA4.

Bassett, C., Cameron, L., Hartmann, M., Hills, M., Karl, I., Morgan, B. and Wessels B. (1997), 'In the Company of Strangers: Users' Perception of the Mobile Phone', in Haddon, L. (ed.) *Communications on the Move: The Experience of Mobile Telephony in the 1990s*, COST248 Report, Farsta: Telia.

Bennett, T. and Watson, J. (2002), *Understanding Everyday Life*, Oxford: Blackwell.

Berg, A-J. (1996), 'Karoline and the Cyborgs: The Naturalisation of a Technical Object', in Frissen, V. (ed.) *Proceedings from COSTA4 Granite Workshop Gender, ICTs and Everyday Life: Mutual Shaping Processes*, Amsterdam, 8–11 February, 6, Brussels: COSTA4.

——and Aune, M. (eds) (1993), *Proceedings from COSTA4 Workshop Domestic Technology and Everyday Life: Mutual Shaping Processes*, Trondheim, Norway: Centre for Technology and Society, University of Trondheim, 28–30 November.

Bergman, S. and van Zoonen, L. (1999), 'Fishing with False Teeth: Women, Gender and the Internet', in Downey, J. and McGuigan, J. (eds) *Technocities*, Sage: London.

Bittman, M. (1998), *The Land of the Lost Weekend? Trends in Free Time among Working Age Australians, 1974–1992*, http://www.sprc.unsw.edu.au/papers/dp83.htm

——and Wajcman, J. (2000), 'The Rush Hour: The Character of Leisure Time and Gender Equity', *Social Forces*, 79(1): 165–89.

Bolter, J. and Grushin, R. (1999), *Remediation: Understanding New Media*, Cambridge, MA: MIT Press.

Boneva, B., Kraut, R. and Frohlich, D. (2001), 'Using E-mail for Personal Relationships: The Difference Gender Makes', *American Behavioral Scientist*, 45(3): 530–49.

Bovill, M. and Livingstone, S. (2001), 'Bedroom Culture and the Privatization of Media Use', in Livingstone, S. and Bovill, M. (eds) *Children and their Changing Media Environment: A European Comparative Study*, Mahwah, NJ: Lawrence Erlbaum Associates.

Büchner, P. (1990), 'Das Telefon im Alltag von Kindern', in Forschungsgruppe Telefonkommunikation (ed.) *Telefon und Gesellschaft*, 2, Berlin: Volker Spiess.

Buckingham, D. (1991), 'Intruder in the House: The Regulation of Children's Viewing in the Home', paper presented at the *Fourth International Television Studies Conference*, London, July.

——(1996), *Moving Images: Understanding Children's Emotional Responses to Television*, Manchester: Manchester University Press.

——(2002), 'The Electronic Generation? Children and New Media', in Lievrouw, S. and Livingstone, S. (eds) *The Handbook of New Media: Social Shaping and Social Consequences*, London: Sage.

Bull, M. (2000), *Sounding Out the City: Personal Stereos and the Management of Everyday Life*, Oxford: Berg.

Carmagnat, M-F. (1995), *Les Télécommunications en situation de mobilité, usages et prospective*, CNET PAA/TSA/UST/4141, January.

Cawson, A., Haddon, L. and Miles, I. (1995), *The Shape of Things to Consume: Bringing Information Technology into the Home*, London: Avebury.

Chatto, E. (2001), 'PACT Models of Social Structure: Time, Place, Attributes and Choices', paper presented at the CRIC workshop *Researching Time*, University of Manchester, 19 September.

Chen, W., Boase, J. and Wellman, B. (2002), 'The Global Villagers: Comparing Internet Users and Uses around the World', in Wellman, B. and Haythornthwaite, C. (eds) *The Internet in Everyday Life*, Oxford: Blackwell.

Claisse, G. (1989), 'Telefon, Kommunikation und Geséelleschaft – Daten gegen Mythen', in Forschungsgruppe Telefonkommunikation (ed.) *Telefon und Gesellschaft*, 1, Berlin: Volker Spiess.

——(1997a), 'Communication and Decommunication', in the European Communication Council Report, *Exploring the Limits: Europe's Changing Communication Environment*, Berlin: Springer.

----(1997b), *The Multimedia Galaxy: Patterns and Future Prospects for Household Equipment*, a report for Telecom Italia, Lyon: Telecom Italia.

——(2000), 'Identités masculines et féminines au telephone: des rôles, des pratiques des perception contrastés', *Réseaux*, 18(103): 51–90.

Cockburn, C. and Ormrod, S. (1993), *Gender and Technology in the Making*, London: Sage.

Cole, J. and Robinson, J. (2002), 'Internet Use, Mass Media and Other Activities in the UCLA Data', *IT&Society*, 1(2): 121–33.

Cooper, G. (2000), 'The Mutable Mobile: Social Theory in the Wireless World', paper presented at the *Wireless World* workshop, University of Surrey, 7 April.

——Green, N., Harper, R. and Murtagh, G. (2001), 'Mobile Users – Fixed Society?', paper for the conference *e-Usages*, Paris, 12–14 June.

COST269 Mobility Workgroup (Haddon, L., de Gournay, C., Lohan, M., Östlund, B., Palombini, I., Sapio, B. and Kilegran, M.) (2001), *From Mobile to Mobility: The Consumption of ICTs and Mobility in Everyday Life*, a report for COST269, Farsta, Sweden: COST269.

Cummings, J. and Kraut, R. (2002), 'Domesticating Computers and the Internet', *Information Society*, 18(3): 221–32.

Cummings, J., Butler, B. and Kraut, R. (2002), 'The Quality of Online Social Relationships', *Communications of the ACM*, 45(7): 103–8.

Darier, E. (1998), 'Time to be Lazy: Work, the Environment and Subjectivities', *Time and Society*, 7(2): 193–208.

Dordick, H. and LaRose, R. (1992), *The Telephone in Daily Life: A Study of Personal Telephone Use*, Philadelphia, PA: Temple University.

Douglas, M. and Isherwood, B. (1980), *The World of Goods: Towards and Anthropology of Consumption*, Harmondsworth: Penguin.

Douglas, S. (1986), 'Amateur Operators and American Broadcasting: Shaping the Future of Radio', in Corn, J. (ed.) *Imagining Tomorrow: History, Technology, and the American Future*, Cambridge, MA: MIT Press.

Du Gay, P., Hall, S., Janes, L., Mackay, H. and Negus, K. (1997), *Doing Cultural Studies: The Story of the Sony Walkman*, London: Sage.

Dutton, W. (1996) *Information and Communication Technologies: Visions and Realities*, Oxford: Oxford University Press.

——(1999) *Society on the Line: Information Politics in the Digital Age*, Oxford: Oxford University Press.

Eldridge, M. and Grinter, R. (2001), 'Studying Text Messaging in Teenagers', paper presented at the CHI 2001 workshop on *Mobile Communications: Understanding User, Adoption and Design*, Seattle, WA, 1–2 April.

Eve, M. and Smoreda, Z. (2001), 'Jeunes retraités, réseaux sociaux et adoption des technologies de communication', *Retraité and Société*, 33, 22–51.

Fielding, G. and Hartley, P. (1987), 'The Telephone: The Neglected Medium', in Cashdan, A. and Jordin, M. (eds) *Studies in Communication*, Oxford: Basil Blackwell.

Fischer, C. (1992), *America Calling: A Social History of the Telephone to 1940*, Berkeley, CA: University of California Press.

Forschungsgruppe Telefonkommunikation (1989), *Telefon und Gesellschaft*, 1, Berlin: Volker Spiess.

Fortunati, L. (1997), 'The Ambiguous Image of the Mobile Phone', in Haddon, L. (ed.) *Communications on the Move: The Experience of Mobile Telephony in the 1990s*, COST248 Report, Farsta: Telia.

——(ed.) (1998), *Telecomunicando in Europa*, Milan: Franco Angeli.

——(2001), 'The Mobile Phone: An Identity on the Move', *Personal and Ubiquitous Computing*, 5(2): 85–98.

——(2003), 'Mobile Phone and the Presentation of Self', paper for the conference *Front Stage/Back Stage: Mobile Communication and the Renegotiation of the Social Sphere*, Grimstad, Norway, 22–24 June.

Frissen, V. (ed.) (1996), *Proceedings from COSTA4 Granite Workshop Gender, ICTs and Everyday Life: Mutual Shaping Processes*, Amsterdam, 8–11 February, 6, Brussels: COSTA4.

——(2000), 'ICTs in the Rush Hour of Life', *The Information Society*, 16: 65–75.

Frohlich, D. and Kraut, R. (2003), 'The Social Context of Home Computing', in Harper, R. (ed.) *Inside the Smart Home*, London: Springer.

Frohlich, D., Dray, S. and Silverman, A. (2001), 'Breaking Up is Hard to Do: Family Perspectives on the Future of the Home PC', *International Journal of Human-Computer Studies*, 54: 701–24.

Future European Telecommunications User Home and Work Group (1997), *Blurring Boundaries: When are Information and Communication Technologies Coming Home?*, COST248 Report, Farsta: Telia.

Gant, D. and Kiesler, S. (2001), 'Blurring the Boundaries: Cell Phones, Mobility, and the Line between Work and Personal Life', in Brown, B. Green, N. and Harper, R. (eds) *Wireless World: Social and Interactional Aspects of the Mobile Age*, London: Springer.

Gareis, K. (2002), *The Intensity of Telework in 2002 in the EU, Switzerland and the USA*, Bonn: Empirica.

Garhammer, M. (1998a), 'Time Structure and Time Cultures in Western European Societies under Pressure of Globalization and Modernization – a Study of Germany, UK, Spain and Sweden', paper presented to the XIV World Congress of Sociology, *Social Knowledge: Heritage, Challenges, Prospects*, Montreal, 26 July to 1 August.

——(1998b), 'Time-use, Time-pressure and Leisure Consumption: Old and New Social Inequalities in the Quality of Life in West Germany, UK, Spain and Sweden', paper presented to the XIV World Congress of Sociology, *Social Knowledge: Heritage, Challenges, Prospects*, Montreal, 26 July to 1 August.

Gershuny, J. (2001), *Web-Use and Net-Nerds: A Neo-Functionalist Analysis of the impact of Information Technology in the Home*, working papers of the Institute for Social and Economic Research, paper 2001–25, Colchester: University of Essex, http:www.iser.essex.ac.uk/pubs/workpaps/wp2001.php

Gillespie, A., Richardson, R. and Cornford, J. (1995), *Review of Telework in Britain: Implications for Public Policy*, a report for the Parliamentary Office of Science and Technology, Employment Department: Sheffield, February.

Gillis, J. (1981), *Youth and History: Tradition and Change in Age Relations, 1770–Present*, London: Academic Press.

De Gournay, C. (1996), 'Waiting for the Nomads Mobile Telephony and Social Change', *Réseaux*, 4(2): 333–50.

——(1997), 'C'est personnel... la communication priveé hors de ses murs', *Réseaux*, 5(2): 21–40.

——(1999), 'Travail et communication au foyer: le partage entre vie priveé et vie professionelle', paper for the conference *Usages and Services in Telecommunications*, Arcachon, France, 7–9 June.

——(2002), 'Pretence of Intimacy in France', in Katz, J. and Aakhus, R. (eds) *Perpetual Contact: Mobile Communication, Private Talk, Public Performance*, Cambridge: Cambridge University Press.

——and Smoreda, Z. (2001), 'La Sociabilité téléphonique et son ancrage spatio-temporel', paper for the conference *e-Usages*, Paris, 12–14 June.

——Tarrius, A. and Missaoui, L. (1997), 'The Structure of Communication Usage of Travelling Managers', in Haddon, L. (ed.) *Communications on the Move: The Experience of Mobile Telephony in the 1990s*, COST248 Report, Farsta: Telia.

Gray, A. (1992), *Video-Playtime: The Gendering of a Leisure Technology*, London: Routledge.

Green, N. (2001), 'Information Ownership and Control in Mobile Technologies', paper for the conference *e-Usages*, Paris, 12–14 June.

Haddon, L. (1988a) 'The Home Computer: The Making of a Consumer Electronic', *Science as Culture*, 2: 7–51.

(1988b) 'Electronic and Computer Games', *Screen* 29(2): 52–73.

——(1992), 'Explaining ICT Consumption: The Case of the Home Computer', in Silverstone, R. and Hirsch, E. (eds) *Consuming Technologies: Media and Information in Domestic Spaces*, London: Routledge.

——(1993) 'Interactive Games', in Hayward, P. and Wollen, T. (eds) *Future Visions: New Technologies on the Screen*, London: British Film Institute Publishing.

——(1994), 'The Phone in the Home: Ambiguity, Conflict and Change', paper presented at the COST248 Workshop, *The European Telecom User*, Lund, Sweden, 13–14 April.

——(1997a), 'The Shaping of Communication Practices', paper for the conference *Penser Les Usages*, Arcachon, France, 27–29 May.

——(ed.) (1997b), *Communications on the Move: The Experience of Mobile Telephony in the 1990s*, COST248 Report, Fasta: Telia.

——(1998a), 'Il Controllo della Comunicazione. Imposizione di Limiti all'uso del Telefono', in Fortunati, L. (ed.) *Telecomunicando in Europa*, Milan: Franco Angeli.

——(1998b), *New Dimensions of Social Exclusion in a Telematic Society*, Working Paper 45, Milan: ACTS-FAIR.

——(1998c), *Locating the Virtual Community in the Households of Europe: The UK Report*, a report for NCR Financial Services, London: London School of Economics.

—— (1999a), 'European Perceptions and Use of the Internet', paper for the conference *Usages and Services in Telecommunications*, Arcachon, France, 7–9 June.

—— (1999b) 'Approaches to Understanding Teleworking', *Telektronikk*, 4, Telenor, Oslo: 29–38.

—— (1999c), 'The Development of Interactive Games', in Mackay, H. and O'Sullivan, T. (eds) *The Media Reader: Continuity and Transformation*, London: Sage.

—— (2000a), 'An Agenda for "Mobility in Everyday Life" for ICT Researchers', paper prepared for the COST269 Mobility Workgroup, London: COST269.

—— (2000b), 'Social Exclusion and Information and Communication Technologies: Lessons from Studies of Single Parents and the Young Elderly', *New Media and Society*, 2(4): 387–406.

—— (2000c), *Old and New Forms of Communication: E-mail and Mobile Telephony*, a report for British Telecom, Martlesham: BT.

—— (2002), 'Information and Communication Technologies and the Role of Consumers in Innovation', in McMeekin, A., Green, K., Tomlinson, M. and Walsh, V. (eds) *Innovation by Demand: Interdisciplinary Approaches to the Study of Demand and its Role in Innovation*, Manchester: Manchester University Press.

—— (2003a), 'Research Questions for the Evolving Communications Landscape', paper for the conference *Front Stage/Back Stage: Mobile Communication and the Renegotiation of the Social Sphere*, Grimstad, Norway, 22–24 June.

—— (2003b), 'Domestication and Mobile Telephony', in Katz, J. (ed.) *Machines that Become Us: The Social Context of Personal Communication Technology*, New Brunswick, NJ: Transaction.

Haddon, L. and Lewis, S. (1994), 'The Experience of Teleworking: An Annotated Review', *International Journal of Human Resource Management*, 5(1): 193–223.

—— and Paul, G. (2001), *Design in the ICT Industry: The Role of Users*, in Coombs, R., Green, K., Richards, A. and Walsh, V. (eds) *Technology and the Market: Demand, Users and Innovation*, Cheltenham: Edward Elgar.

—— and Silverstone, R. (1993), *Teleworking in the 1990s: A View from the Home*, SPRU/CICT Report Series, no. 10, University of Sussex, Falmer.

—— and Silverstone, R. (1994), 'The Careers of Information and Communication Technologies in the Home', in Bjerg, K. and Borreby, K. (eds) *Proceedings of the International Working Conference on Home Oriented Informatics, Telematics and Automation*, Copenhagen, 27 June to 1 July, Copenhagen: University of Copenhagen.

—— and Silverstone, R. (1995a) *Lone Parents and their Information and Communication Technologies*, SPRU/CICT Report Series, no. 12, University of Sussex, Falmer.

—— and Silverstone, R. (1995b) *Home Information and Communication Technologies and the Information Society*, a report to the High Level Group of Experts, University of Sussex, Falmer, December.

—— and Silverstone, R. (1996), *Information and Communication Technologies and the Young Elderly*, SPRU/CICT Report Series, no. 13, University of Sussex, Falmer.

——and Silverstone, R. (2000) 'Home Information and Communication Technologies and the Information Society', in Ducatel, K., Webster, J. and Herrmann, W. (eds) *The Information Society in Europe: Work and Life in an Age of Globalization*, Lanham, MD: Rowman and Littlefield.

——and Skinner, D. (1991) 'The Enigma of the Micro: Lessons from the British Home Computer Boom', *Social Science Computer Review*, 9(3): 435–49.

D'Haenens, L. (2001), 'Old and New Media: Access and Ownership in the Home', in Livingstone, S. and Bovill, M. (eds) *Children and their Changing Media Environment. A European Comparative Study*, Mahwah, NJ: Lawrence Erlbaum Associates.

Hampton, K. and Wellman, B. (2001), 'Long Distance Community in the Network Society: Contact and Support beyond Netville', *American Behavioral Scientist*, 45(3): 477–96.

Hartmann, M. (2003) *The (De)Construction of Users, Morals and Consumption*, EMTEL2 Key Deliverable, SMIT, Brussels, http://www.emtel2/org/.

Häußermann, H. and Petrowsky, W. (1989), 'Die Bedeutung des Telefons für Arbeitslose', in Forschungsgruppe Telefonkommunikation (ed.) *Telefon und Gesellschaft*, 1, Berlin: Volker Spiess.

Haythornthwaite, C. (2001a), 'Online Personal Networks: Size, Composition and Media Use among Distance Learners', *New Media and Society*, 2(2): 195–226.

——(2001b), 'The Internet in Everyday Life', *American Behavioral Scientist*, 45(3): 363–82.

Horrigan, J. and Rainie, L. (2002a), *Getting Serious Online*, Pew Internet and American Life Project, http://www.pewinternet.org/.

Horrigan, J. and Rainie, L. (2002b), *The Broadband Difference*, Pew Internet and American Life Project, http://www.pewinternet.org/.

Horrigan, J., Rainie, L., Allen, K., Madden, M. and O'Grady, E. (2003), *The Ever-Shifting Internet Population: A New Look of Internet Access and the Digital Divide*, Pew Internet and American Life Project, http://www.pewinternet.org/.

Howard, P., Rainie, L. and Jones, S. (2001), 'Days and Nights on the Internet: The Impact of a Diffusing Technology', *American Behavioral Scientist*, 45(3): 383–404.

Howard, P., Rainie, L. and Jones, S. (2002), 'Days and Nights on the Internet', in Wellman, B. and Haythornthwaite, C. (eds) *The Internet in Everyday Life*, Oxford: Blackwell.

Ito, M. and Daisuke, O. (2003), 'Mobile Phones, Japanese Youth and the Replacement of Social Contact', paper for the conference *Front Stage/Back Stage: Mobile Communication and the Renegotiation of the Social Sphere*, Grimstad, Norway, 22–24 June.

James, A. and Prout, A. (eds) (1997), *Constructing and Reconstructing Childhood: Contemporary Issues in the Sociological Study of Children*, London: Falmer Press.

Jansen, J. (1993), 'Commuting: Home Sprawl, Job Sprawl and Traffic James', in

Salomon, I., Bovy, P. and Orfeuil, J. (eds) *A Billion Trips a Day: Tradition and Transition in European Travel Patterns*, Dordrecht: Kluwer Academic Press.

Jauréguiberry, F. (1997), 'L'usage du téléphone portatif comme expérience sociale', *Réseaux*, 5(2): 149–64.

Johnsen, T. (2003), 'The Social Context of the Mobile Phone Use of Norwegian Teens', in Katz, J. and Aakhus, R. (eds) *Perpetual Contact: Mobile Communication, Private Talk, Public Performance*, Cambridge: Cambridge University Press.

Johnson, L. (1982–3), *Images of Radio: The Construction of the Radio by Popular Radio Magazines*, Melbourne Working Paper no. 4, Department of Education, University of Melbourne.

Johnsson-Smaragdi, U. (2001), 'Media Use Styles among the Young', in Livingstone, S. and Bovill, M. (eds) *Children and their Changing Media Environment: A European Comparative Study*, Mahwah, NJ: Lawrence Erlbaum Associates.

Jouet, J. (2000), 'Retour critique sur la sociologie des usage', *Réseaux*, 100: 486–521.

Jung, J-Y., Qui, J. and Kim, Y-C. (2001), 'Internet Connectedness and Inequality: Beyond the "Divide"', *Communications Research*, 28(4): 507–35.

Kanayama, T. (2003), 'Ethnographic Research on the Experience of Japanese Elderly People Online', *New Media and Society*, 5(3): 267–88.

Kasesniemi, E. and Rautianen, P. (2002), 'Mobile culture of children and teenagers in Finland', in Katz, J. and Aakhus, R. (eds) *Perpetual Contact: Mobile Communication, Private Talk, Public Performance*, Cambridge: Cambridge University Press.

Katz, J. (ed.) (2003), *Machines that Become Us: The Social Context of Personal Communication Technology*, New Brunswick, NJ: Transaction.

——and Aakhus, R. (eds) (2002), *Perpetual Contact: Mobile Communication, Private Talk, Public Performance*, Cambridge: Cambridge University Press.

——and Aspden, P. (1998), 'Internet Dropouts in the USA: The Invisible Group', *Telecommunications Policy*, 24(4/5): 327–39.

——and Rice, R. (2002a), 'Syntopia: Access, Civic Involvement and Social Interaction on the Internet', in Wellman, B. and Haythornthwaite, C. (eds) *The Internet in Everyday Life*, Oxford: Blackwell.

——and Rice, R. (2002b), *Social Consequences of Internet Use: Access, Involvement and Interaction*, Boston, MA: MIT Press.

——Rice, R. and Aspden, P. (2001), 'The Internet, 1995–2000: Access, Civic Involvement and Social Interaction', *American Behavioral Scientist*, 45(3): 405–17.

Kavanaugh, A. and Patterson, S. (2001), 'The Impact of Community Computer Networks on Social Capital and Community Involvement', *American Behavioral Scientist*, 45(3): 496–509.

Kiesler, S., Lundmark, V., Zdaniuk, B. and Kraut, R. (2000), 'Troubles with the Internet: The Dynamics of Help at Home', *Human Computer Interaction*, 14(4): 323–51.

Kingsley, P. and Anderson, T. (1998), 'Facing Life without the Internet', *Internet Research: Electronic Networking Applications and Policy*, 8(4): 303–12.

Klamer, L., Haddon, L. and Ling, R. (2000), *The Qualitative Analysis of ICTs and Mobility, Time Stress and Social Networking*, report of EURESCOM P-903, Heidelberg.

Kraut, R., Patterson, M., Lundmark, V., Kiesler, S., Mukhopadhyay, T. and Scherlis, W. (1998), 'Internet Paradox: A Social Technology that Reduces Social Involvement and Psychological Well-Being?', *American Psychologist*, 53(9): 1017–31.

Kraut, R., Mukhopadhyay, T., Szczypula, J., Kiesler, S. and Scherlis, W. (2000), 'Communication and Information: Alternative Uses of the Internet in Households', *Information Systems Research*, 10: 287–303.

Kraut, R., Kiesler, S., Boneva, B., Cummings, J., Helgeson, V. and Crawford, A. (2002), 'Internet Paradox Revisited', *Journal of Social Issues*, 58: 49–74.

Kraut, R., Kiesler, S., Boneva, B. and Shklovski, I. (2003), 'Examining the Impact of Internet Use: Details Make a Difference', paper given at the workshop *Domestic Impact of Information and Communication Technologies*, Estes Park, Colorado, 5–8 June, available at http://www-2.cs.cmu.edu/~kraut, /ict/abstracts.html.

Lacohée, H. and Anderson, B. (2001), 'Interacting with the Telephone', *International Journal of Human-Computer Studies*, 54(5): 665–99.

Lally, E. (2002), *At Home with Computers*, Oxford: Berg.

Lee, S. (1999), 'Private Uses in Public Spaces: A Study of an Internet Café', *New Media and Society*, 1(3): 331–50.

Lelong, B. and Beaudouin, V. (2001), 'Usages d'Internet, nouveaux terminaux et hauts debits: premier bilan après quatre années d'expérimentations', paper for the conference *e-Usages*, Paris, 12–14 June.

Lelong, B. and Thomas, F. (2001), 'L'Apprentissage de l'Internaute: socialisation et autonomisation', paper for the conference *e-Usages*, Paris, 12–14 June.

Lemish, D. and Cohen, A. (2003), 'Tell Me How You Use Your Mobile and I'll Tell You Who You Are: Israelis Talk about Themselves', paper for the conference *Front Stage/Back Stage: Mobile Communication and the Renegotiation of the Social Sphere*, Grimstad, Norway, 22–24 June.

Lenhart, A., Rainie, L. and Lewis, O. (2001), *Teenage Life Online: The Rise of Instant Messaging and the Internet's Impact on Friendship and Family Relationships*, http://www.pewinternet.org/ 20 June.

Leung, L. and Wei, R. (1999), 'Who are the Mobile Phone Have-Nots? Influences and Consequences', *New Media and Society*, 1(2): 209–26.

Licoppe, C. and Heurtin, J-P. (2001), 'Managing One's Availabilty to Telephone Communication through Mobile Phones: A French Case Study of the Development Dynamics of Mobile Phone Use', *Personal and Ubiquitous Computing*, 5(2): 99–108.

Licoppe, C. and Heurtin, J-P. (2002), 'France: Preserving the Image', in Katz, J. and Aakhus, R. (eds) *Perpetual Contact: Mobile Communication, Private Talk, Public Performance*, Cambridge: Cambridge University Press.

Lie, M. and Sørensen, K. (eds) (1996), *Making Technologies Our Own? Domesticating Technology into Everyday Life*, Oslo: Scandinavian University Press.

Ling, R. (1997), '"One Can Talk about Common Manners!" The Use of Mobile Telephones in Inappropriate Situations', in Haddon, L. (ed.) *Communications on the Move: The Experience of Mobile Telephony in the 1990s*, COST248 Report, Farsta: Telia.

——(1998), '"It's OK to be Available": The Use of Traditional and Mobile Telephony among Norwegian Youth', paper presented to the XIV World Congress of Sociology *Social Knowledge: Heritage, Challenges, Prospects*, Montreal, 26 July to 1 August.

——(2000), 'Direct and Mediated Interaction in the Maintenance of Social Relationships', in Sloane, A. and van Rijn, F. (eds) *Home Informatics and Telematics: Information, Technology and Society*, Dordrecht: Kluwer Acadmic Press.

——(2004, *The Mobile Connection: The Cell Phone's Impact on Society*, San Francisco, CA: Morgan Kaufmann.

——and Haddon, L. (2003), *Mobile Telephony, Mobility and the Coordination of Everyday Life*, in Katz, J. (ed.) *Machines that Become Us: The Social Context of Personal Communication Technology*, New Brunswick, NJ: Transaction.

——and Helmersen, P. (2000), '"It Must be Necessary, it has to Cover a Need": The Adoption of Mobile Telephony among Pre-adolescents and Adolescents', paper presented at the seminar *Sosiale Konsekvenser av Mobiltelefoni*, organized by Telenor, Oslo.

——and Thrane, K. (2001), '"It actually separates us a little bit, but I think that is an Advantage": The Management of Electronic Media in Norwegian Households', paper for the conference *e-Usages*, Paris, 12–14 June.

——and Yttri, B. (2002), 'Hyper-Coordination via Mobile Phones in Norway', in Katz, J. and Aakhus, R. (eds) *Perpetual Contact: Mobile Communication, Private Talk, Public Performance*, Cambridge: Cambridge University Press.

——Julsrud, T. and Kroug, E. (1997), 'The Goretex Principle: The Hytte and Mobile Telephones in Norway', in Haddon, L. (ed.) *Communications on the Move: The Experience of Mobile Telephony in the 1990s*, COST248 Report, Farsta: Telia.

Livingstone, S. (1997), 'Mediated Childhoods: A Comparative Approach to Young People's Changing Media Environment in Europe', *European Journal of Communication*, 13(4): 435–56.

——(2001), *Online Freedom and Safety for Children*, IPPR/Citizens Online Research Publication, 3, November.

——(2002), *Young People and New Media*, London: Sage.

——(2003), 'Children's Use of the Internet: Reflections on the Emerging Research Agenda', *New Media and Society*, 5(2): 147–66.

——and Bober, M. (2003), *UK Children go Online: Listening to Young People's Experiences*, London, Media@LSE, http://www.children-go-online.net.

——and Bovill, M. (1999), *Young People, New Media*, London: London School of Economics.

——and Bovill, M. (2001a), *Children and their Changing Media Environment: A European Comparative Study*, Mahwah, NJ: Lawrence Erlbaum Associate.

——and Bovill, M. (2001b), *Families and the Internet: An Observational Study of Children and Young People's Internet Use*, a report for BTexact Technologies, London School of Economics.

Lohan, M. (1997), 'No Parents No Kids Allowed: Telecoms in the Individualist Household', in The Future European Telecommunications User Home and

Work Group, *Blurring Boundaries: When are Information and Communication Technologies Coming Home?*, COST248 Report, Farsta: Telia.

Manceron, V. (1997), 'Get Connected! Social Uses of the Telephone and Modes of Interaction in a Peer Group of Young Parisians', in The Future European Telecommunications User Home and Work Group, *Blurring Boundaries: When are Information and Communication Technologies Coming Home?*, COST248 Report, Farsta: Telia.

——Leclerc, C., Houdart, S., Lelong, B. and Smoreda, Z. (2001), 'Processus de hiérarchisation au sein des relations sociales et diversification des modes de communication au moment de la naissance d'un premier enfant', paper for the conference *e-Usages*, Paris, 12–14 June.

Mansell, R. and Steinmuller, W.E. (2000), *Mobilizing the Information Society: Strategies for Growth and Opportunity*, Oxford: Oxford University Press.

Mante-Meijer, E., Haddon, L., Concejero, P., Klamer, L., Heres, J., Ling, R., Thomas, F., Smoreda, Z. and Vrieling, I. (2001), *Checking it out with the People – ICT Markets and Users in Europe*, a report for EURESCOM, Heidelberg, available at http://www.eurescom.de/public/projects/P900–series/p903/default.asp.

Marsh, A and Mullins, D. (1998), 'The Social Exclusion Perspective and Housing Studies: Origins, Applications and Limitations', *Housing Studies*, 13(6): 749–59.

Martin, O. and de Singly, F. (2000), 'L'Evasion amicable: l'usage du téléphone familial par les adolescents', *Réseaux*, 18(103): 91–118.

Mercier, P. (2001), 'Nouveux moyens de communication interpersonelle et partage des rôles en matière de sociabilité au sein des couples', paper for the conference *e-Usages*, Paris, 12–14 June.

Mesch, G. (2003), 'The Family and the Internet: The Israeli Case', *Social Science Quarterly*, 84(4): 1038–50.

Miller, D. and Slater, D. (2000), *The Internet: An Ethnographic Approach*, Oxford: Berg.

Millerand, F., Giroux, L., Piette, J. and Pons, C. (1999), 'Les Usages d'Internet chez les adolescents québécois', paper for the conference *Usages and Services in Telecommunications*, Arcachon, France, 7–9 June.

Miyata, K., Boase, J., Wellman, B. and Ikeda, K. (2003), 'The Mobile-izing Japanese: Connecting to the Internet by PC and Webphone in Yamanashi', paper for the conference *Front Stage/Back Stage: Mobile Communication and the Renegotiation of the Social Sphere*, Grimstad, Norway, 22–24 June.

Moyal, A. (1989), 'The Feminine Culture of the Telephone: People, Patterns and Policy', *Prometheus*, 7(1): 5–31.

Nafus, D. and Tracey, K. (2002), 'Mobile Phone Consumption and Concepts of Personhood', in Katz, J. and Aakhus, R. (eds) *Perpetual Contact: Mobile Communication, Private Talk, Public Performance*, Cambridge: Cambridge University Press.

National School Boards Foundation (2001), *Safe and Smart: Research and Guidelines for Children's Use of the Internet*, http:www.nsbf.org/safe-smart/full-report.htm.

Neustadtl, A. and Robinson, J. (2002), 'Media Use Differences between Internet Users and Nonusers in the General Social Survey, *IT&Society*, 1(2): 100–20.

Nie, N. (2001), 'Sociability, Interpersonal Relations and the Internet: Reconciling Conflicting Findings', *American Behavioral Scientist*, 45(3): 420–35.

——and Erbring, L. (2002), 'Internet and the Mass Media: A Preliminary Report', *IT&Society*, 1(2): 134–41.

——Hillygus, D. and Erbring, L. (2002), 'Internet Use, Interpersonal Relations and Sociability: A Time Diary Study', in Wellman, B. and Haythornthwaite, C. (eds) *The Internet in Everyday Life*, Oxford: Blackwell.

Nilles, J., Carson, F., Gray, P. and Hanneman, G. (1976), *The Telecommunications–Transportation Trade-Off*, Chichester: Wiley.

O'Hara, K., Sellan, A., Brown, B. and Perry, M. (2000), 'Exploring the Relationship between Mobile Phone and Document Use during Business Travel', paper presented at the *Wireless World* workshop, University of Surrey, Guildford, 7 April.

Oksman, V. and Rautianinen, P. (2001), 'Mobile Communication of Children and Teenagers Finland 1997–2000', paper for the conference *e-Usages*, Paris, 12–14 June.

Östlund, B. (1999) *Images, Users, Practices: Senior Citizens Entering the IT Society*, KFB-report 1999, Stockholm: Swedish Board for Transport and Communication Research.

Palen, L., Salzman, M. and Youngs, E. (2001), 'Discovery and Integration of Mobile Communications in Everyday Life', *Personal and Ubiquitous Computing*, 5(2): 109–22.

Pasquier, D. (2001), 'Media at Home: Domestic Interactions and Regulation', in Livingstone, S. and Bovill, M. (eds) *Children and their Changing Media Environment: A European Comparative Study*, Mahwah, NJ: Lawrence Erlbaum Associates.

——Buzzi, C., d'Haenens, L. and Sjoberg, U. (1998), 'Family Lifestyles and Media Use Patterns: An Analysis of Domestic Media among Flemish, French, Italian and Swedish Children and Teenagers', *European Journal of Communication*, 13(4): 503–19.

Perin, P. (1994), *Consumer Telephone Usage*, paper given at COST248 meeting, Lund, Sweden, March.

Plant, S. (2002), *On the Mobile: The Effects of Mobile Telephones on Social and Individual Life*, London: Motorola.

Potier, F., Turel, A. and Orfeuil, J-P. (1993), 'Travelling across Europe: Going for Pleasure and Profit', in Salomon, I., Bovy, P. and Orfeuil, J. (eds) *A Billion Trips a Day: Tradition and Transition in European Travel Patterns*, Dordrecht: Kluwer Academic Press.

Punie, Y. (1997), 'Imagining "Non-Users": Rejection of ICTs in Flemish Households', paper given at the conference *Penser Les Usages*, Arcachon, France, 27–29 May.

Rainie, L. (2001), 'Technology and the Social World of American Teens', presentation at the workshop *Domesticating the Internet, Commercializing the Family: A Comparative Look at Families, the Internet and Issues of Privacy*, Haifa, 4–6 June.

Rakow, L. (1988), 'Women and the Telephone: The Gendering of a Communications Technology', in Kramarae, C. (ed.) *Technology and Women's Voices: Keeping in Touch*, London: Routledge and Kegan Paul.

——and Navaro, V. (1993), 'Remote Mothering and the Parallel Shift: Women Meet the Cellular Phone', *Critical Studies in Mass Communication*, 10(2): 144–57.

Ribak, R. and Turow, J. (2003), '"Internet Power and Social Context": A Globalization Approach to Web Privacy Concerns', *Journal of Broadcasting and Electronic Media*, 47(3): 328.

Rice, R. (2002), 'Primary Issues in Internet Use: Access, Civic and Community Involvement, and Social Interaction and Expression', in Lievrouw, L. and Livingstone, S. (eds) *The Handbook of New Media: Social Shaping and Consequences*, London: Sage.

Rivère, C. and Licoppe, C. (2003), 'From Voice to Text: Continuity and Change in the use of Mobile Phones in France and Japan', paper for the conference *Front Stage/Back Stage: Mobile Communication and the Renegotiation of the Social Sphere*, Grimstad, Norway, 22–24 June.

Roberts, K. (1976), 'The Time Famine', in Parker, S. (ed.) *The Sociology of Leisure*, London: Allen and Unwin.

Robinson, J. and Godbey, G. (1999), *Time for Life: The Surprising Ways Americans Use their Time*, 2nd edn, University Park, PA: Penn State University Press.

Robinson, J., Kestnbaum, M., Neustadtl, A. amd Alvarez, A. (2002), 'The Internet and Other Uses of Time', in Wellman, B. and Haythornthwaite, C. (eds) *The Internet in Everyday Life*, Oxford: Blackwell.

Rommes, E. (2002), *Gender Scripts and the Internet: The Design and Use of Amsterdam's Digital City*, Enschede: Twente University Press.

——(2003), '"I Don't Know How to Fit it into my Life": The Gap between Inclusion Initiatives and the Personal Stories of the Excluded', paper presented at the EMTEL conference, *New Media and Everyday Life in Europe*, London, 23–26 April.

Rössler, P. (2001), 'Between On-line Heaven and Cyberhell: The Framing of "the Internet" by Traditional Media Coverage in Germany', *New Media and Society*, 3(1): 49–66.

Russo, A-M. (2003) 'New Media in Single Parent Households: Practices and Identity Formation in Relation to Public Discourses of Technology', paper presented at the EMTEL conference, *New Media and Everyday Life in Europe*, London, 23–26 April.

Salomon, I. and Tacken, M. (1993), 'Taming the Peak: Time and Timing as Travel Moderators', in Salomon, I., Bovy, P. and Orfeuil, J. (eds) *A Billion Trips a Day: Tradition and Transition in European Travel Patterns*, Dordrecht: Kluwer Academic Press, 53–74.

Salomon, I., Bovy, P. and Orfeuil, J. (eds) (1993), *A Billion Trips a Day: Tradition and Transition in European Travel Patterns*, Dordrecht: Kluwer Academic Press.

Scannel, P. (1988), 'Radio Times: The Temporal Arrangements of Broadcasting in the Modern World', in Drummond, P. and Paterson, R. (eds) *Television and its Audience: International Perspectives*, London: British Film Institute.

Segalen, M. (1999), 'La Téléphone des familles', *Réseaux* 17(96): 15–44.

Sennett, R. (1986), *The Fall of Public Man*, London: Faber and Faber.

Shotton, M. (1989), *Computer Addiction: A Study of Computer Dependency*, London: Taylor and Francis.

Silverstone, R. (1993), 'Time, Information and Communication Technologies in the Household', *Time and Society*, 2(3): 283–311.

——(1994), *Television and Everyday Life*, London: Routledge.

——(1995), 'Media, Communication, Information and the "Revolution" of Everyday Life', in Emmott, S. (ed.) *Information Superhighways: Multimedia Users and Futures*, London: Academic Press.

——and Haddon, L. (1995), *Social Aspects of Advanced Communication Technologies and Services: Issues, Analyses and Cases*, paper for ACTS-FAIR, Falmer: University of Sussex.

——and Haddon, L. (1996a), *Television, Cable and AB Households: A Report for Telewest*, University of Sussex, Falmer, August.

——and Haddon, L. (1996b), 'Design and the Domestication of Information and Communication Technologies: Technical Change and Everyday Life', in Silverstone, R. and Mansell, R. (eds) *Communication by Design: The Politics of Information and Communication Technologies*, Oxford: Oxford University Press.

——Hirsch, E. and Morley, D. (1992), 'Information and Communication Technologies and the Moral Economy of the Household', in Silverstone, R. and Hirsch, E. (eds) *Consuming Technologies*, London: Routledge.

Simmel, G. (1997), 'The Metropolis and Mental Life', in Frisby, D. and Featherstone, M. (eds) *Simmel on Culture*, London: Sage.

Singh, S. (2001), 'Gender and the Use of the Internet in the Home', *New Media and Society*, 3(4): 395–416.

Skelton, F. (1989), 'Teenagers and the Telephone', in Forschungsgruppe Telefonkommunikation, *Telefon und Gesellschaft*, 1, Berlin: Volker Spiess.

Skinner, D. (1994), 'Computerised Homes: Visions and Realities', in Bjerg, K. and Borreby, K. (eds) *Proceedings of the International Working Conference on Home Orientated Informatics, Telematics and Automation*, Copenhagen, 27 June to 1 July, Copenhagen: University of Copenhagen.

Smoreda, Z. and Licoppe, C. (1999), 'La Téléphonie résidentielle de foyers: réseaux de sociabilité et cycle de vie', paper for the conference *Usages and Services in Telecommunications*, Arcachon, France, 7–9 June.

Smoreda, Z. and Thomas, F. (2001), 'Social Networks and Residential ICT Adoption and Use', *EURESCOM Summit 2001 3G Technologies and Applications*, Heidelburg, 12–15 November.

Sørensen, K. (1994), *Technology in Use: Two Essays on the Domestication of Artefacts*, Senter for Teknologi og Samfunn, Trondheim.

——(1999), *Rush-Hour Blues of the Whistle of Freedom? Understanding Modern Mobility*, STS-Working Paper, Senter for Teknologi og Samfunn, Trondheim, March.

Southerton, D. (2001), '"Squeezing Time": Allocating Practices, Co-ordinating Networks and Scheduling Society', paper for conference *Spacing and Timing*, Palermo, Italy, 1–3 November.

Spigel, L. (1992), *Make Room for TV: Television and the Family Ideal in Postwar America*, Chicago: University of Chicago Press.

Taylor, A. and Harper, R. (2001a), 'Talking "Activity": Young People and Mobile Phones', paper presented at CHI 2001 workshop, *Mobile Communications: Understanding User, Adoption and Design*, Seattle, 31 March to 5 April.

Taylor, A. and Harper, R. (2001b), *The Gift of the Gab? A Design Oriented Sociology of Young People's Use of 'MobilZe!'* working paper, Digital World Research Centre, University of Surrey, UK, available at http://www.surrey.ac.uk/dwrc/papers.html.

Thomas, F. and Mante-Meijer, E. (2001), 'Internet Haves and Have Nots in Europe', paper for the conference *e-Usages*, Paris, 12–14 June.

Thomas, G. and Wyatt, S. (2000), 'Access is not the only Problem: Using and Controlling the Internet', in Wyatt, S., Henwood, F., Miller, N. and Senker, P. (eds) *Technology and In/equality, Questioning the Information Society*, London: Routledge.

Townsend, A. (2001), 'Mobile Communication in the Twenty-First Century City', in Brown, B., Green, N. and Harper, R. (eds) *Wireless World; Social and Interactional Aspects of the Mobile Age*, London: Springer.

Tracey, K. (1999), *Interacting with Systems: The Forgotten Network*, BTexact Research Report, Martlesham: BTexact.

Turkle, S. (1984), *The Second Self: Computers and the Human Spirit*, London: Granada.

——(1988), 'Computational Reticence: Why Women Fear the Intimate Machine', in Kramerae, C. (ed.) *Technology and Women's Voices*, London: Routledge.

——(1996), *Life on the Screen: Identity in the Age of the Internet*, London: Weidenfeld and Nicolson.

Turner, J. and Grieco, M. (2000), 'Gender and Time Poverty: The Neglected Social Policy Implications of Gendered Time, Travel and Transport', *Time & Society*, 9(1): 129–36.

Turow, J. and Nir, L. (2000), *The Internet and the Family 2000: The View from the Parents, the View form the Kids*, report from The Annenberg Public Policy Center, University of Pennsylvania, Philadelphia, PA.

UCLA Center for Communication Policy (2000), *The UCLA Internet Report: 'Surveying the Digital Future'*, http://www.ccp.ucla.edu/pages/internet-report. asp.

Urry, J. (2000), *Sociology beyond Societies: Mobilities for the Twenty-First Century*, London: Routledge.

Van Dusseldorp, M., Haddon, L. and Paul, G. (1998), *Design for All and ICT Business Practice*, a report for TIDE, EC, Delft: TIDE.

Vestby, G. (1994), 'Constructing Childhood: Children Interacting with Technology', in Berg, A. and Aune, M. (eds) *Proceedings from COSTA4 Workshop Domestic Technology and Everyday Life: Mutual Shaping Processes*, 28–30 November, Centre for Technology and Society, Trondheim, Norway: University of Trondheim.

Ward, K. (2003), *An Ethnographic Study of Domestic Internet Consumption in a Costal Town*, EMTEL2 Deliverable, Dublin, http://www.emtel2/org/.

Warschauer, M. (2003), *Technology and Social Inclusion: Rethinking the Digital Divide*, Cambridge, MA: MIT Press.

Watt, S., Lea, M. and Spears, R. (2002), 'How Social is Internet Communication? A Reappraisal of Bandwidth and Anonymity Effects', in Woolgar, S. (eds) *Virtual Society? Technology, Cyperbole and Reality*, Oxford: Oxford University Press.

Weilenmann, A. and Larsson, C. (2001), 'Local Use and Sharing of Mobile Phones', in Brown, B., Green, N. and Harper, R. (eds) *Wireless World: Social and Interactional Aspects of the Mobile Age*, London: Springer.

Wellman, B. (1992), 'Which Ties and Networks Give What Support', *Advances in Group Processes*, 9: 207–35.

—— (1999), 'The Network Community', in Wellman, B. (ed.) *Networks in the Global Village*, Boulder, CO: Westview.

—— and Haythornthwaite, C. (eds) (2002), *The Internet in Everyday Life*, Oxford: Blackwell.

—— Quan Hase, A., Witte, J. and Hampton, K. (2001), 'Does the Internet Increase, Decrease or Supplement Social Capital? Social Networks, Participation and Community Commitment', *American Behavioral Scientist*, 45(3): 437–56.

White, C. and Scheb II, J. (2000), 'Impact of Media Messages about the Internet: Internet Anxiety as a Factor in the Adoption Process in the USA', *New Media and Society*, 2(2): 181–94.

Williams, R. (1974), *Television: Technology and Cultural Form*, London: Routledge.

Winston, B. (1989), 'The Illusion of Revolution', in Forester, T. (ed.) *Computers in Human Context: Information Technology, Productivity and People*, Oxford: Basil Blackwell.

Wyatt, S., Thomas, G. and Terranova, T. (2002), 'They Came, They Surfed, They Went Back to the Beach: Conceptualising Use and Non-Use of the Internet', in Woolgar, S. (ed.) *Virtual Society? Technology, Cyperbole and Reality*, Oxford: Oxford University Press.

Yoon, K. (2002), 'Extending Familialism through the Mobile: Young People's Re-articulation of Traditional Sociality through Mobile Phones in Seoul, South Korea', paper presented at the Third Wireless World Conference, *The Social Shaping of Mobile Futures Location! Location!*, University of Surrey, Guildford, 17–18 July.

Yung, V. (2003), 'Ideotechnic Values of the Mobile Phone: An Analysis of Media Representation in Hong Kong', paper for the conference *Front Stage/Back Stage: Mobile Communication and the Renegotiation of the Social Sphere*, Grimstad, Norway, 22–24 June.

Index

balance of time spent on different
  activities, 159
behaviour in public spaces,
  109–10, 160
experience of mobility, 107–8,
  112, 160
experience of time, 92, 94–5, 160
managing mobility, 105–6, 112
managing time, 87, 95–7
parents monitoring children, 39,
  160
sociability, 68, 71, 159
social networks, 160
uneven experience of ICTs, 6, 20,
  159
social construction of childhood,
  see childhood, social construction
  of
social construction of parenthood,
  see parenthood, social
  construction of
social exclusion, 3, 6, 13, 20
social networks, 6, 8–9, 83n3
  domestication in 74–76
  phone calls, 58
  supporting ICT acquisition and
    use, 71–74
  see also sociability, social
    networks and the Internet;
    sociability, mobile phone;
    youth, peers
social shaping of technology, 135
  media influence, 137–8, 150
  social discourses, 136–7, 150

technological seepage, 121
telebanking, 88, 103
telephone, 21–3, 78
  children, 37–8, 40, 43–4, 56–7,
    95
  complaints about calls, 59, 68n6

cordless phones, 58
cost of calls, 56–7, 59, 68n3
filtering calls, 59–60
gender, 44, 61–4, 124–5
intrusiveness, 57, 59
locating in the home, 58, 152n12
representations, 136
retired, 127–8
services, 148
teleworkers, 120
unemployed, 118–19
teleshopping, 88, 103–4
television, 23, 64
  cable, 24, 90, 98n4
  children, 34, 36, 42
  locating in the home, 152
  satellite 24, 145
telework, 103
teleworkers, 83n2, 117, 132n2
  acquiring ICTs, 119, 131
  managing ICTs, 57–8, 120–1,
    131
  support networks, 73
teletext, 147
texting, 45–9, 51n6, 90
time, 6, 9, 64
  disposable, 87–8
  fragmented, 91, 97
  leisure, 94
  multitasking, 91–2
  planning, 95–7
  quality, 93–5
  -shifting ICTs, 88
  spontaneity, 95–7
  stress, 87, 92–3, 97, 98n7
  timing of ICT use, 88–91, 97

unemployed, 21–2, 118–19
uneven experience of ICTs, 67
  access to ICTs, 6, 17
  adoption of ICTs, 6